I0464107

HANDILAW GUIDE:

TRADEMARKS

ROBERT GOOZNER

ISBN:
ISBN-13: 9781543188929

DEDICATION

To my wife Nena and my son Jake.

HANDILAW GUIDE: TRADEMARKS

TABLE OF CONTENTS

HANDILAW GUIDE: TRADEMARKS

INTRODUCTION

Welcome to the world of trademarks. Trademarks is a fascinating and complicated field that is difficult to comprehend. Most books on the field are dense tomes that seem designed to frighten off someone who wants to obtain a basic working knowledge of the topic. One may assume that trademarks cannot be understood except by a person with deep knowledge in the field.

However, someone working in business and industry, or a non-specialized legal professional can obtain a good overview of trademarks in a fairly rapid fashion. Also, people outside of the United States will need to better understand American trademarks in order to do business in this country.

This book is aimed for these people. The basic aspects of trademarks are laid out in a simple and concise manner. Reading this book will take no more than a couple of hours and leave the reader with a basic introduction into the field. Also, this book can serve as a first go-to reference.

We hope that you find this book to be enlightening.

Robert E. Goozner
Managing Partner – Trademarks Department
Young & Thompson International Patent and Trademark Law
Alexandria, Virginia
www.young-thompson.com

HANDILAW GUIDE: TRADEMARKS

SECTION 1: WHAT IS A TRADEMARK?

1 WHAT IS A TRADEMARK?

A trademark is an indication of the origin or source of the goods or services. It serves to product the public from confusion in the marketplace. That is, the function of a trademark is to exclusively identify the commercial source or origin of products or services, so a trademark indicates source or serves as a badge of origin. In other words, trademarks serve to identify a particular business as the source of goods or services. The utilization of a trademark in this way is known as trademark use. Certain exclusive rights attach to a registered mark.

Trademark rights generally arise out of the use of, or to maintain exclusive rights over, the mark in relation to certain products or services, assuming there are no other trademark objections.

What is United State Law?

Many of the people reading this are not familiar with United States law. People from places like Europe and the far east frequently find United States law puzzling due to its hybrid nature. A short review of United States law would be helpful to those trying to understand American trademarks.

There are four branches of United States law, which are 1) constitutional law, 2) legislative law, 3) administrative law and 4) common law.

Constitutional law is law that is grounded in the United States Constitution. The United States Constitution does not mention trademarks. However, most intellectual property rights find their basis in Section 8, Article 8 of the United States Constitution, which states that Congress shall have power to "promote the progress of science and useful arts, by securing for limited times to authors and inventors the exclusive right to their respective writings and discoveries." Regarding trademarks, this combines with Section 8, Article 1 which covers to "provide for the . . .general welfare of the United States."

The next aspect of the law is legislative law, which must be passed by both houses of Congress and signed by the President of the United States. This yields the present Federal trademarks laws, which are enshrined in the Lanham Act, which is also called the Trademark Act and Title 15 of United States Code (U.S.C.)

Administrative law is the rules that the appropriate Federal agency sets base on legislative law. In the United States these rules are set by the United States Patent and Trademark Office (USPTO) . The trademark rules can be found in Title 37 of the Code of Federal Regulations (C.F.R.).

The final branch of the law is common law, which is law that is found by the courts. Most (but not all) trademark litigation is in the Federal Courts, which includes District Courts, The Court of Appeal of the Federal Circuit and the United States Supreme Court. When these cases are discussed, they are referred to by their citations, which indicate the court, date and reference of the decision. An example of a citation is: In re Tam, 785 F.3d 567 (Fed. Cir. 2015). This citation gives the name of the case (In re Tam), the legal volume where it can be found (785 F.3d 567), and the court and the date (Fed. Cir. (Court of Appeal of the Federal Circuit) 2015). Detailed explanations of citations can be found in The Bluebook – A Uniform System of Citation, published by The Harvard Law Review Association.

Why Should You Have A Trademark?

Trademarks play an invaluable role in protecting consumers

and in promoting global economic growth. Trademarks enable purchases to make quick, confident and safe purchasing decisions. Trademarks promote freedom of choice. Trademarks and related intellectual property encourage vibrant competition for the benefit of consumers, workers, brand owners and society.

A trademark is a simple route for your customers to find you. In a crowded market it is difficult to distinguish your produce from competitors. Trademarks/brands are an efficient commercial communication tool to capture customer attention and make your business, products and services stand out.

A trademark lets you advantageously use social media and the internet. With good name recognition, your brand will be a keyword that a potential customer enter into a search engine or social media platform (Facebook, Twitter, Pinterest., etc.) when looking for your products and services.

Unlike other forms of intellectual property like patents and copyright, Trademarks never expire. Your trademark will not expire as long as you are using it in United States commerce. Some of the most recognized brands in the United States today have been around for over a hundred years. The Ford oval trademark was first registered in 1907. Coca-Cola was registered in 1886. Listerine was first registered in 1879.

Trademarks are a valuable asset. Trademarks appreciate in value over time. The more your business reputation grows, the more valuable your brand will be. Trademarks have value as property, similar to patents, machinery and real estate, that can be bought, sold, licensed or used as a security interest to secure a loan.

What Are The Types Of Trademarks?

A trademark is a word, graphic, package design, logo or any combination of them that can be used to distinguish the goods or services.

A trademark can be a **brand name** identifying the goods. An example is Coca Cola:

A trademark can be trade dress, which is color, graphics, packaging, shape of the goods, or with sufficient use of the goods themselves. An example of this would be the Jello package:

A **service mark** identifies services. An example would be a law firm service mark:

A certification mark identifies goods or services meeting specified qualifications:

A collective mark identifies the goods and services of a collective organization:

What Are The Forms Of Trademarks?

Trademarks can take many forms. They can be words, symbols, colors, sounds of combinations of these as long as they indicate the source of the goods. The hybrid quality can be seen in many well-known trademarks, including the Michelin Man, the Golden Arches, etc.

Can Sounds Be Trademarks?

Sounds can be trademarked too. An example is the three chimes of the NBC television network.

See
https://www.uspto.gov
/trademarks/soundmar
ks/72349496.mp3

MGM's roaring lion is also a trademark:

See
https://www.uspto.gov
/trademarks/soundmar
ks/73553567.mp3

In this case both the graphic (which can move) and the sound is a trademark.

The USPTO lists additional examples of sound trademarks on its website at: https://www.uspto.gov/trademark/soundmarks/trademark-sound-mark-examples.

Can Colors Be Trademarks?

In the right context, a color can be a trademark. An example is the red sole of a Louboutin shoe. However, in this case, there must be a contrast with the rest of the shoe. If the shoe is entirely red, there is no trademark protection.

Louboutin trademark shoe.   YSL red shoe.

The contrast requirement was based on the drawing and the specimen filed in the USPTO:

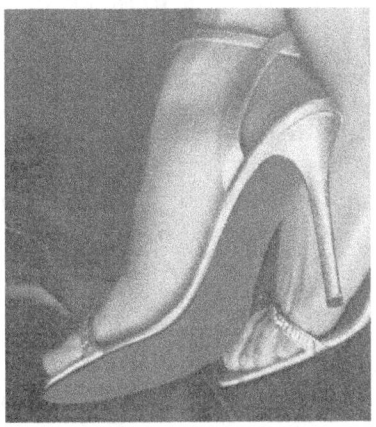

Drawing   Specimen

Sometimes a color can't be used as a trademark, for example black for boat motors. See Brunswick Corp. v. British Seagull Ltd., 35 F.3d 1527 (Fed. Cir. 1994). The criteria were set by the United States Supreme Court in Qualitex Co. v. Jacobson Products Co., 514 U.S. 159 (1995). In the Qualitex decision, the Court held that the greenish-gold color of dry cleaning press pads was protectable as a trademark. This color met the requirements of a trademark by acting as a symbol, operating as a source identifier and serving no other function aside from identifying the press pads' source.

Another example is pink for fiberglass insulation. in its

decision. See In re Owens-Corning Fiberglas Corp., 744 F.2d 1116 (Fed. Cir. 1985). Here, the Federal Circuit determined the color pink could be a trademark based on evidence that included use of the color for 29 years, over $42 million in advertising expenditures and a survey demonstrating 50 percent consumer recognition of the source of the applicant's pink insulation.

State And Federal Trademarks?

A quirk of United States law is that a trademark can either be registered nationally or in a state-by-state basis. A federal registration, under the Lanham Act, gives the registrant rights throughout the entire United States and its territories and possessions; a state registration gives the registrant trademark rights only within the territory of the state.

State trademark applications are filed with a state's trademark authority. For example, the State of New York, registers trademarks under the Department of State, Division of Corporations, State Records and UCC. See http://www.dos.ny.gov/corps/staterecordsfaq.html.

On the other hand, a federal trademark registration is issued by the United States Patent and Trademark Office. A federal trademark registration is available only for marks used in interstate commerce or commerce between the United States and another country.

One may also apply for federal registration before actual use of the mark, based on intent to use. Purely intrastate use of a mark—that is, within only one state—is not sufficient to obtain a federal trademark registration. Intrastate use is sufficient, however, for registration of a trademark in that state.

In the modern interconnected world the selling of goods or services only in one state is very rare. As a result, one considering trademark protection should always go the Federal route.

What Are The Trademark Symbols?

If a trademark is unregistered means the owner is merely asserting that he or she has a trademark under common law. The symbol for this type of trademark is TM, which is usually superscripted as TM.

Registered trademarks are indicated using the registered trademark symbol (®) In some jurisdictions it is unlawful or illegal to use the ® symbol with a mark which has not been registered.

A service mark (a trademark for the provision of services) is denoted by SM, superscripted as [SM]. The service mark symbol is less commonly used than the trademark symbol, especially outside the United States.

2 GEOGRAPHICAL INDICATION

1.0 OVERVIEW

A OC-AOP is the French (and European) system which designate origin, know-how and quality indications to identify products rooted in their lands, i.e., the French "terroir."

The L'Appellation d'Origine Protégée (AOP), also called the protected designation of origin (PDO) refers to a product whose main production steps are carried out according a recognized expertise in the same geographical area, which gives its characteristics to the product. It is a European sign which protects the product name throughout the European Union.

The Appellation d'Origine Contrôlée (AOC) refers to products meet the criteria of the PDO and protects the name on French territory. It is a step towards the PDO, which is the European Union sign now. It can also involve products not covered by European regulations (case of forest products for example).

This is the concept of "terroir" which founded the concept of AOP.

A terroir is a particular area where production takes its originality by directly specifying its production area. This is a space within which the local community built, during its history, a collective know-how of production. The terroir is based on a system of interactions between the physical and the biological environment, and a set of human factors. There are originality and characteristics of the product.

The rules of developing a PDO are listed in specifications and are subject to control procedures, implemented by an independent body approved by INAO (Institute National de L'Origine et de la Qualité).

The origin of AOC-AOP was historically the fight against fraud that has built gradually in French law from the beginning of the twentieth century (Law of 1905), using the designations of origin concept. A decree in 1935 on the protection of the wine market created the appellation of controlled origin (Appellation d'Origine Contrôlée (AOC)), applicable to wines and spirits, and the body responsible for defining, their protection and control. The field was opened to all agricultural and food products in 1990.

Later, the French agricultural model inspired the development of an EU regulation, which established in 1992 the concept of AOP, the European equivalent of AOC, for products other than wines and spirits, and extended to wines in 2009. Since then, the PDO concerns all European wine and food products including production, processing and preparation are performed in a specific geographical area, using recognized know-how and particular specifications.

This was further developed to offer clarification to the consumer. Since January 1, 2012, once registered at European level, the products concerned must bear the designation PDO, and only wines are allowed to bear the designation of origin French control (AOC).

2.0. PRODUCTS

Here are some current (2012) numbers:

Food products and dairy products include 49 dairy products under AOC (mainly cheese). There was a 1.5 billion Euros turnover, 16% of the production of cheeses in France. Production was estimated at 187,429 tonnes of food products: fruits, vegetables and olive oils. 42 food designations are under AOC AOC with an impact of about 150 million Euros.

Regarding wine products, 364 wines and brandies are under protection with an impact of 14 billion euros. This includes over 80% of French wine production covering 59.8% of the total area of vines

The turnover in 2012 included AOP food: 170 million euros, dairy PDOs: 1750 million Euros, and AOP wines and spirits - 16 000 million Euros.

Consider wine. A wine bottle conveys a lot of information:

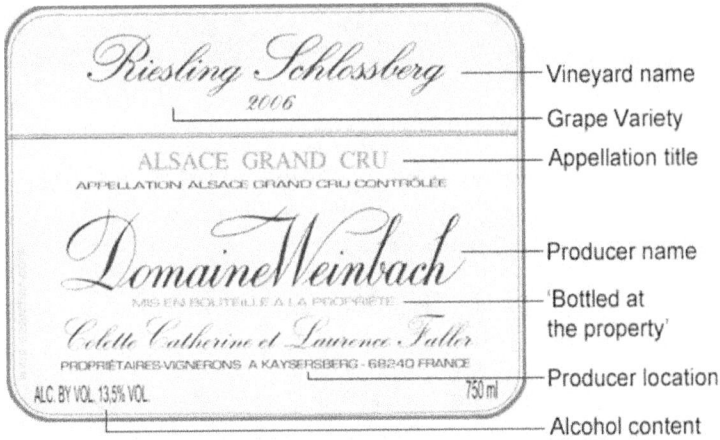

Note that the appellation can only be 25% of the height of the title.

An example of cheese is Roquefort:

A Bresse chicken must still have its head on and costs almost

20 Euros per kilo. Butter, olives, apples; all can have an AOP designation.

AOC/AOP has five guarantees:

1) The production area is geographically delimited inside of a wine region according to traditional criteria, but also from geological, soil factors related to terroir.

2) The grapes are selected to make the best wine on a specific terroir, depending on weather conditions.

3) The yield per hectare is fixed by decree. Maximum efficiency which, in any case, exceed the standard. We talk hectoliters per hectare (hl/ha). How to grow and maintain vines is also regulated.

4) The minimum alcohol content, apart, of course, any added sugar.

5) The cultivation and vinification processes with a concern to preserve traditional winemaking practices.

3.0. PROTECTED DESIGNATION OF ORIGIN (PDO-AOC)

These are the red (dark) and yellow (light) labels:

The Protected designation of origin (PDO) is the name of an area, a specific place or, in exceptional cases, the name of a country, used as a designation for an agricultural product or a foodstuff. PDO signifies that the product comes from such an area, place or country, whose quality or properties are significantly or exclusively determined by the geographical environment, including natural and human factors. Production, processing and preparation all take place within the determined geographical area.

In other words, to receive the PDO status, the entire product must be traditionally and entirely manufactured (prepared, processed and produced) within the specific region and thus acquire unique properties.

4.0 PROTECTED GEOGRAPHICAL INDICATION (PGI-IGP)

The blue (dark) and yellow label (light) is the junior varsity of PDO-AOC:

The Protected geographical indication (PGI) is the name of an area, a specific place or, in exceptional cases, the name of a country, used as a description of an agricultural product or a foodstuff. This guarantees that the product comes from such an area, place or country which has a specific quality, goodwill or other characteristic property, attributable to its geographical origin. Production, processing or preparation takes place within the determined geographical area.

In other words, to receive the PGI status, the entire product must be traditionally and at least partially manufactured (prepared, processed or produced) within the specific region and thus acquire unique properties.

5.0 TRADITIONAL SPECIALITIES GUARANTEED (TSG-STG)

The label is blue (dark) and yellow (light):

The TSG quality scheme aims to provide a protection regime for traditional food products of specific character. Differing from PDO and PGI, this quality scheme does not certify that the protected food product has a link to specific geographical area.

To qualify for a TSG a food must be of "specific character" and either its raw materials, production method or processing must be "traditional." Under Art. 3 of Regulation 1151/12 "specific character" is defined as "the characteristic production attributes which distinguish a product clearly from other similar products of the same category". Under Art. 3 of Regulation 1151/12 "traditional" is defined as "proven usage on the domestic market for a period that allows transmission between generations; this period is to be at least 30 years". For a food name to be registrable under the TSG scheme it must (a) have been traditionally used to refer to the specific product; or (b) identify the traditional character or specific character of the product.

A TSG creates an exclusive right over the registered product name. Accordingly, the registered product name can only be used by producers who conform to the registered production method and product specifications.

"The legal function of the TSG is to certify that a particular agricultural product objectively possesses specific characteristics which differentiate it from all others in its category, and that its raw materials, composition or method of production have been consistent for a minimum of 30 years. Thus, TSG food denominations are registered trade signs with a distinctive function." Art. 3 of Regulation 1151/12.

6.0 OTHER LABELS

The Label Rouge is a particularly French designation:

Label Rouge (Red Label) is a sign of quality assurance in France as defined by Law No. 2006-11 (January 5, 2006).

Products eligible for the Label Rouge are food items (including seafood) and non-food and unprocessed agricultural products such as flowers. According to the French Ministry of Agriculture: "The Red Label certifies that a product has a specific set of characteristics establishing a superior level to that of a similar current product"

The green and white AB label stands for bio agriculture:

AB excludes the use of synthetic chemicals, genetically modified organisms and respects natural balances. AB certifies and organic product.

7.0 GEOGRAPHICAL INDICATION PROTECTION IN THE UNITED STATES

"Geographical indications" ("GIs") are defined at Article 22(1) of the World Trade Organization's (WTO) 1995 Agreement on Trade Related Aspects of Intellectual Property Rights (TRIPS) as "indications which identify a good as originating in the territory of a Member, or a region or locality in that territory, where a given quality, reputation or other characteristic of the good is essentially attributable to its geographic origin."

Examples of geographical indications from the United States include: "FLORIDA" for oranges; "IDAHO" for potatoes; and "WASHINGTON STATE" for apples.

Geographical indications can be viewed as a subset of trademarks. Geographical indications serve the same functions as trademarks, because like trademarks they are: 1) source-identifiers, 2) guarantees of quality, and 3) valuable business interests.

The United States has found that by protecting geographical indications through the trademark system – usually as certification and collective marks -- the United States can provide TRIPS-plus levels of protection to GIs, of either domestic or foreign origin.

The United States has provided protection to foreign and domestic GIs since at least 1946, decades prior to the implementation of the TRIPS Agreement (1995) when the term of art "geographical indication" came into wide use.

The United States' GI system uses administrative trademark structures already in place, and provides opportunities for any interested party to oppose or cancel a registered GI if that party believes that it will be damaged by the registration or continued existence of a registration. The same governmental authority (the United States Patent and Trademark Office or "USPTO") processes applications for both trademarks and GIs.

GI's are used as certification marks.

The U.S. Trademark (Lanham) Act provides that geographic

names or signs--which otherwise would be considered primarily geographically descriptive and therefore unregistrable as trademarks or collective marks without a showing of acquired distinctiveness in the United States--can be registered as certification marks.

A certification mark is any word, name, symbol, or device used by a party or parties other than the owner of the mark to certify some aspect of the third parties' goods/services.

There are three types of certification marks used to indicate:

1) Regional or other origin.

2) Material, mode of manufacture, quality, accuracy or other characteristics of the goods or services.

3) That the work or labor on the goods/services was performed by a member of a union or other organization.

An example of this is ROQUEFORT.

The mark ROQUEFORT (U.S. Registration No. 571,798) is used to indicate that the cheese has been manufactured from sheep's milk and cured in the caves of the Community of Roquefort (France) in accordance with their long established methods and processes.

There are two important characteristics of sCertification Marks:

1) The owner does not use it.

2) The certification mark does not indicate a commercial source or distinguish the goods or services of one person from those of another person.

Geographical indications also are protected through common law trademark law without being registered by the USPTO. For example, the Trademark Trial and Appeal Board (TTAB) has held that "COGNAC" is protected as a common-law (unregistered) certification mark in the United States. *Institut National Des Appellations v. Brown-Forman Corp*, 47 USPQ2d 1875, 1884(TTAB 1998) ("Cognac" is a valid common law regional certification mark, rather than a generic term, since purchasers in the United States primarily understand the "Cognac" designation to refer to brandy originating in the Cognac region of France, and not to brandy produced elsewhere, and since opposer's control and limit use of the designation which meets certain standards of regional origin.)

8.0 GOATS DO ROAM

Goats do Roam had Reg. No. 2885533. The mark was owned by Fairview Trust of South Africa. The mark was opposed by Bully Hill Vinyard, which manufactured "Goat Red Wine" claiming a likelihood of confusion. Bully Hills Marks included LOVE MY GOAT, LE GOAT, BULLY HILL BILLY GOAT, HAPPY HEARD, GOAT WHITE WINE, GOAT POWER, WLATERS HIS NAME GOATS HIS GAME, KING OF THE GOATS

Not all of Bully Hills' marks were in the original complaint

The Opposer tried to amend and consolidate proceedings but was refused on grounds of timeliness.

The issue was settled out of court – Stipulation of dismissal April 2004. This can all be found in the TESS database in the Patent Office's web site.

Goat Roti had Reg. No. 3822182, which was published for opposition on January 8, 2002. The Opposer was the French institute Institute National des Appellations d'Origine ("INAO"), and claimed likelihood of confusion with "Cotes du Rhône." This too was settled out of court.

These proceedings can be found at the registration number in TESS.

9.0 JPK PARIS 75

In re Miracle Tuesday, LLC, 695 F.3d 1339 (Fed. Cir 2012).

The question is: Is the mark identified with Paris as source of the goods? The label says "Paris," but is there any connection with Paris.

Under Section 2(e)(3) of the Lanham Act, a mark may not be registered on the principal register if the mark, "when used on or in connection with the goods of the applicant is primarily geographically deceptively misdescriptive of them." 15 U.S.C. § 1052(e)(3). A mark is primarily geographically deceptively misdescriptive, and thus barred from registration, if: (1) "the primary significance of the mark is a generally known geographic location"; (2) "the consuming public is likely to believe the place identified by the mark indicates the origin of the goods bearing the mark, when in fact the goods do not come from that place"; and (3) "the misrepresentation was a material factor in the consumer's decision" to purchase the goods. In re Cal. Innovations, Inc., 329 F.3d 1334, 1341(Fed.Cir.2003).

The issue is materiality. JPK is not located in Paris, but in Miami. Paris is renowned for fashion

Found: "Because we have determined that the primary significance of Paris to the relevant public is the geographic place, and in view of the renown and reputation of fashion designs originating in Paris, we may infer that at least a substantial portion of consumers who encounter applicant's mark featuring the word "Paris" on applicant's products are likely to be deceived into believing that those products come from or were designed in Paris."

A similar case is *In re California Innovations, Inc.*, 329 F.3d 1334 (Fed. Cir . 2003). In this case, the products (bags and wraps) did not originate in California. The PTO Examiner refused registration of an ITU as being primarily geographically misdescriptive. Applicant appealed to Court of Appeal of the Federal Circuit (CAFC) (Judge Rader).

The Lanham Act 1052(a):

No trademark by which the goods of the applicant may be distinguished from the goods of others

shall be refused registration on the principal register on account of its nature unless it—

(a) Consists of or comprises immoral, <u>deceptive,</u> or scandalous matter; or matter which may disparage or falsely suggest a connection with persons, living or dead, institutions, beliefs, or national symbols, or bring them into contempt, or disrepute; <u>or a geographical indication which, when used on or in connection with</u>

<u>wines or spirits, identifies a place other than the origin of the goods</u> and is first used on or in connection with wines or spirits by the applicant on or after one year after the date on which the WTO Agreement (as defined in section3501(9) of title 19) enters into force with respect to the United States."

The test is that the PTO must establish that (1) the mark misrepresents or misdescribes the goods, (2) the public would likely believe the misrepresentation, and (3) the misrepresentation would materially affect the public's decision to purchase the goods.

The two categories of marks are: (1) primarily geographically descriptive, (2) deceptively misdescriptive.

In re Nantucket required set forth a goods-place association requirement, where the Court required a geographically deceptively misdescriptive mark to have more than a merely a primary geographic connotation. The issue related to shirts manufactured in North Carolina and did not originate in Nantucket Island. In re Nantucket, 677 F.2d 95 (C.P.P.A. 1982)

Under NAFTA a geographically deceptive misdescription could no longer acquire distinctiveness.

The current test is deceptiveness.

10.0 DESCRIPTIVENESS

An example is AMERICAN.

If "AMERICA" or "AMERICAN" appears in a phrase or slogan, the examining attorney must evaluate the entire mark to determine whether it is merely descriptive as laudatory or even incapable. In re Boston Beer Co. L.P., 198 F.3d 1370, 53 USPQ2d 1056 (Fed. Cir. 1999) (THE BEST BEER IN AMERICA so highly laudatory and descriptive as applied to beer and ale that it is incapable of acquiring distinctiveness).

In re Carvel Corp., 223 USPQ 65 (TTAB 1984) (AMERICA'S FRESHEST ICE CREAM was held incapable of registration for ice cream); In re Wileswood, Inc., 201 USPQ 400

(TTAB 1978) (AMERICA'S BEST POPCORN! and AMERICA'S FAVORITE POPCORN!) was merely descriptive of unpopped popcorn.

Typically, these marks primarily extol the quality or popularity of the goods or services and secondarily denote geographic origin. The examining attorney must look at each mark to determine whether it is capable, considering all relevant circumstances and case law. TMEP 1209.03(n).

Other examples are as follows:

"National", "International", "Global" and "Worldwide." Function or purpose includes source or provider of goods and services, retail store or distributor services, slogans, repetition of descriptive or generic term and punctuation. Examples include: "Best Beer in America," "National Rent a Fence," "Screenwipe," "La Lingerie," "Tires Tires Tires," "Ceasar! Ceaser!," "888 Patents," (phone number), and "Hotels.com."

11.0 REFERENCES

http://www.dico-du-vin.com/a/aocaop-appellation-dorigine-controleeappellation-dorigine-protegee/

https://en.wikipedia.org/wiki/Geographical_indications_and_traditional_specialities_in_the_European_Union

www.agriculture.gouv.fr

http://www.uspto.gov/sites/default/files/web/offices/dcom/olia/globalip/pdf/gi_system.pdf.

3 WHAT CAN'T BE A TRADEMARK 1
THE CATEGORIZATION MATRIX

Trademarks are highly useful. Unlike a patent a trademark can last forever. Alternatively, a trademark can be lost if it is not aggressively protected. Patents, protect technology and those who develop technology, but a trademark is directed at apprising the public of the source of the goods. However, not everything can be trademarked. This chapter covers the categorization of things that can and can't be trademarked.

1.0 TRADEMARKS AND THE LANHAM ACT

As was reviewed in the first chapter, trademarks are grounded in the Lanham Act, 15 U.S.C., which is also referred to as the Trademark Act. A trademark is an indication of the origin or source of the goods or services:

- Words

- Symbol

- Color

- Sound

Examples of trademarks include Coca Cola, the Michelin Man,

the Golden Arches, etc.

Even sounds can be trademarked:

See http://www.uspto.gov/trademark/soundmarks/trademark-sound-mark-examples.

2.0 WHAT CAN'T BE TRADMARKED?

What can't be a trademarked? This is covered in Section 1052 of the Lanham Act:

15 U.S.C. §1052

(a) Consists of or comprises immoral, deceptive, or scandalous matter; or matter which may disparage or falsely suggest a connection with persons, living or dead, institutions, beliefs, or national symbols, or bring them into contempt, or disrepute; or a geographical indication which, when used on or in connection with wines or spirits, identifies a place other than the origin of the goods and is first used on or in connection with wines or spirits by the applicant on or after one year after the date on which the WTO Agreement (as defined in section 3501(9) of title 19) enters into force with respect to the United States.

(b) Consists of or comprises the flag or coat of arms or other insignia of the United States, or of any State or municipality, or of any foreign nation, or any simulation thereof.

(c) Consists of or comprises a name, portrait, or signature identifying a particular living individual except by his written consent, or the name, signature, or portrait of a deceased President of the United States during the life of his widow, if any, except by the written consent of the widow.

(d) Consists of or comprises a mark which so resembles a mark registered in the Patent and Trademark Office, or a mark or trade name previously used in the United States by another and not abandoned, as to be likely, when used on or in connection with the goods of the applicant, to cause confusion, or to cause mistake, or to deceive: Provided, That if the Director determines that confusion, mistake, or deception is not likely to result from the continued use by more than one person of the same or similar marks under conditions and limitations as to the mode or place of use of the marks or the goods on or in connection with which such marks are used, concurrent registrations may be issued to such persons when they have become entitled to use such marks as a result of their concurrent lawful use in commerce prior to . . .

3.0 SECONDARY MEANING

Entwined with this is the concept of secondary meaning.

Secondary meaning is defined in 15 U.S.C. §1052(f):

Except as expressly excluded in subsections (a), (b), (c), (d), (e)(3), and (e)(5) of this section, nothing herein shall prevent the registration of a mark used by the applicant which has become **distinctive of the applicant's goods** in commerce. The Director may accept as *prima facie* evidence that the mark has become distinctive, as used on or in connection with the applicant's goods in commerce, proof of substantially exclusive and continuous use thereof as a mark by the applicant in commerce for the five years before the date on which the claim of distinctiveness is made.

The purpose and significance of secondary meaning may be described as follows:

"A term which is descriptive . . . may, through usage by one producer with reference to his product, acquire a special significance so that to the consuming public the word has come to mean that the product is produced by that particular manufacturer." 1 Nims, Unfair Competition and Trademarks at §37 (1947). This is what is known as secondary meaning.

"The crux of the secondary meaning doctrine is that the mark comes to identify not only the goods but the source of those goods. To establish secondary meaning, it must be shown that the primary significance of the term in the minds of the consuming public is not the product but the producer (citations omitted). This may be an anonymous producer, since consumers often buy goods without knowing the personal identity or actual name of the manufacturer." *Ralston Purina Co. v. Thomas J. Lipton, Inc.,* 341 F. Supp. 129, 133, 173 USPQ 820, 823 (S.D.N.Y. 1972).

4.0 TRADMARK CATEGORIES

The categories of secondary meaning are as follows:

1) Generic

2) Descriptive

3) Suggestive

4) Arbitrary or Fanciful

This list is from weakest to strongest, where Generic is the weakest and Arbitrary or Fanciful is the strongest.

A generic trademark is merely a word or words that describes the goods, i.e., can be found in the dictionary. The primary meaning of a generic trademark becomes the product or service itself rather than an indication of source for the product or service. Sometimes a trademark can enter the language if not sufficiently protected and the right to the trademark is lost. Heroin, thermos and aspirin are examples of trademarks which were lost by entering the language in the United States.

A descriptive trademark describes either the goods or the characteristics of the goods. This type of mark must have a distinctive character. That is, there must be secondary meaning associated with the mark.

A suggestive mark suggests a meaning or relationship but does not describe the goods themselves. A suggestive trademark tends to indicate the nature, quality, or a characteristic of the products or services in relation to which it is used, but does not describe this characteristic, and requires imagination on the part of the consumer to identify the characteristic. Suggestive marks invoke the consumer's perceptive imagination. An example of a suggestive mark is COPPERTONE or BLU-RAY.

An arbitrary or fanciful trademark is usually a common word which is used in a meaningless context (e.g. "SANKA" for coffee). Such marks consist of words or images which have some dictionary meaning before being adopted as trademarks, but which are used in connection with products or services unrelated to that dictionary meaning. Arbitrary marks are also immediately eligible for registration.

For example, consider donuts.

DONUTS

The naked generic word "DONUTS" is the weakest and cannot be trademarked, while the incorporation of fanciful elements into Dunkin Donuts and Krispy Kreme make them distinctive enough to be a trademark.

So for the category Generic: A genus of which the particular product is a species. Generic is merely descriptive of an article or its qualities, ingredients or characteristics. Exceptions: - has acquired secondary meaning or use over time.

The category Descriptive is defined in Section 2 of the Lanham Act:

(f) Except as expressly excluded in subsections (a), (b), (c), (d), (e)(3), and (e)(5) of this section, nothing herein shall prevent the registration of a mark used by the applicant which has become distinctive of the applicant's goods in commerce. The Director may accept as prima facie evidence that the mark has become distinctive, as used on or in connection with the applicant's goods in commerce, proof of substantially exclusive and continuous use thereof as a mark by the applicant in commerce for the five years before the date on which the claim of distinctiveness is made.

The category Suggestive is neither exactly descriptive on one hand nor truly fanciful on the other. If a term is suggestive, it is entitled to registration without proof of secondary meaning.

The category Fanciful or Arbitrary enjoy all the rights accorded to suggestive terms as marks – without the need of debating whether the term is 'merely descriptive' and with ease of establishing infringement. See Abercrombie & Fitch v. Hunting World, *Inc.*, 537 F.2d 4 (2d Cir. 1976).

For example, the following of themselves give no indication

of the products they represent:

However, one may note that Exxon was once Esso which was once Standard Oil, which had a significant impact on antitrust law.

5.0 QUICK PRINT

In re Quik-Print Copy Shops, 616 F.2d 523 (C.C.P.A. 1980)

This case was an appeal to the C.C.P.A. of the Examiner's refusal to grant a trademark to "QUIK-PRINT". Appellant argued that "Quick" and "Print" used individually are well known mundane names useful to the trade, the term "QUIK-PRINT" is a fanciful and distinctive term not ordinarily usable in the trade to describe any quality, characteristic or ingredient of the service. Court noted that "QUICK-PRINT" = "QUIK-PRINT", and the appellant also used the term "Same Day Service" in advertising. Appellant argued that "mental gymnastics" used by the Examiner and Court proved that mark is suggestive.

The Court found that the mark was merely descriptive. The Court found "nothing in this record to establish that applicant has achieved a recognition or secondary meaning in the mark "QUIK-PRINT."

6.0 BEANIE BABIES

Ty Inc. V Ruth Perryman (2001 WL 826893 (N.D. Ill.)

Motion for Summary Judgment

Ty sells collectable toys under the names of BEANIE BABIES, THE BEANIE BABYS COLLECTION, BEANIE BUDDIES COLLECTION, BEANIE BUDDIES etc.

Ruth Perryman established Bargain Beanies business to serve the second hand market. Sells only "retired" Bargain Beanies. Ty sued for trademark infringement. Ty had not registered the mark "Beanies"

The Lanham Act protects a mark against infringement by "colorable imitations" which "likely to cause confusion, or to cause mistake or to deceive" consumers as to the source of the goods.

Important points are "Beanies" is an important component of the mark. "Bargain" is a significant part of the mark. A disclaimer of not being affiliated with Ty on Perryman's web site reduced likelihood of confusion. Also, Ty has created a unique product

"Taking all of these factors together, we believe that reasonable minds can differ as to whether the marks are sufficiently similar to create a likelihood of confusion . . . but there remains a genuine question of fact as to whether the similarity in the products creates a likelihood of confusion."

The next issue was: is "Beanies" generic?

Perryman claimed "Beanies" generic citing bean bags and bean bag chairs. Ty claimed fanciful using dictionary definitions of beanies worn by collegians.

The Court found that Ty had a strong mark and found "beanie" to be descriptive rather than suggestive, arbitrary and fanciful. The Court found defendant's evidence of genericness "to be sparse at best."

This brings us back to the issue of secondary meaning. In this case there were articles referring to Beanie Babies as "Beanies", tags and boxes. Neither party offered consumer testimony. A consumer survey submitted by Ty, but was recent and not representative of consumer understanding at the time.

Based on strength of the mark, the Court found summary judgment of dilution by the defendants use of the word "Beanies."

7.0 AFTERMATH

Kyriakos Tsiolis v. Interscope Records, Aftermath Entertainment, and Andre Young (aka Dr. Dre) 946 F.Supp (N.D. Ill. 1996)

This was a motion for a preliminary injunction. The fact pattern was that Tsiolis organized heavy metal band called Aftermath. He even obtained an Illinois mark for "Aftermath." Also a Service mark "Aftermath" was registered at USPTO. He distributed about 2,500 copies of "Words That Echo Fear" album. His second album did worse and sold 162 copies of "Eyes of Tomorrow."

Page 35

They also gave 33 live performances. So the band was raking in about $5,000 per year. From this, it is clear that Tsiolis had reached the point in his Rock and Roll career where one might consider getting a haircut and applying for a real job.

Enter Dr. Dre, the well-known rapper:

Dr. Dre dissociated from Death Row Records. He Chose "Aftermath" to symbolize the split from Death Row. The split and new label were reported in Vibe and LA Times. He had a promotional plan, an ad in Billboard and posters. About $200,000 was spent on production, distribution and marketing.

The dictionary defines aftermath as "the period immediately following a usually ruinous event." See, e.g., Merriam-Webster.

Also, the Rolling Stones had an album before Tsiolis held the mark:

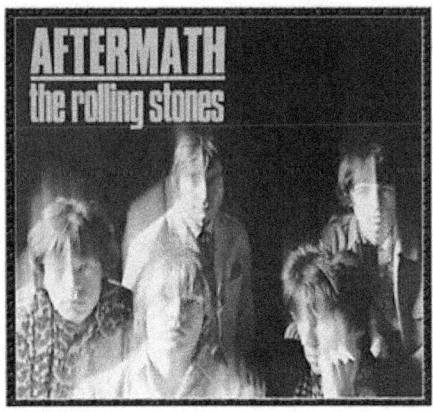

Expert witnesses were called in.

Tsiolis' expert Prof. Weinstein opined lines separating genres of music are ever changing and there was considerable "melding together" of rock and rap.

Dr. Dre's Expert Fred Bronson asserted heavy metal is for teenage white working class males and rap is for young urban black males, and that the two genres of music are played on different radio stations.

Gary Arnold of Best Buy testified that there are separate "rock" and "rap sections.

The Court's findings:

The registration of "Aftermath" is *prima facie* valid. The Court noted the 5 categories of distinctiveness: generic, descriptive, suggestive, arbitrary and fanciful.

A generic term, though registered with the USPTO, receives no protection under federal and state trademark law, citing *Door Sys. V. Pro-line Door Sys.*, 83 F.3d 169, 171 (7th Cir. 1996). Neither party argued that "Aftermath" was generic. "aftermath" was in lower case in dictionary. Even if descriptive, there is no "secondary meaning" in the "music world". There was no evidence proffered of likelihood of confusion.

The factors:

1) similarity of the services.

2) area and manner of concurrent use.

3) strength of the mark.

4) degree of similarity of marks in appearance and suggestion.

5) degree of care likely to be exercised by the consumers.

6) intent by the alleged infringer to "palm off" its services as that as another.

7) evidence of actual confusion.

Held: no evidence of actual confusion, appearance and suggestion of the two marks are dissimilar, no intent to "palm off", "Aftermath" is <u>weak</u>, consumers likely to use a high degree of care, no likelihood of confusion demonstrated.

The Court-ordered injunction would cost the defendant (Dr. Dre) about $400,000.

The injunction was accordingly denied.

"Likelihood of confusion is frequently a disputed issue upon which reasonable minds can differ. . . Tsiolis will have his day in court."

8.0 PATENTS.COM

In re Oppedahl & Larsen, *LLP*, 373 F.3d 1171 (Fed Cir. 2004)(Judge Rader)

The Trademark Trial and Appeal Board (TTAB) aff'd USPTO's refusal to register patents.com as being merely descriptive under the Lanham Act.

TMEP 1209.03(m):

"Because TLD's generally serve no source indicating function, their addition to an otherwise unregistrable mark typically cannot render it registrable."

Consider TMEP 1209.03:

Because TLDs generally serve no source-indicating function, their addition to an otherwise unregistrable mark typically cannot render it registrable. In re 1800Mattress.com IP LLC, 586 F.3d 1359, 92 USPQ2d 1682 (Fed. Cir. 2009) (MATTRESS.COM generic for "online retail store services in the field of mattresses, beds, and bedding," and applicant "presented no evidence that ".com" evoked anything but a commercial internet domain"); In re Hotels.com, L.P., 573 F.3d 1300, 91 USPQ2d 1532 (Fed. Cir. 2009) (HOTELS.COM generic for "providing information for

Page 39

others about temporary lodging; [and] travel agency services, namely, making reservations and bookings for temporary lodging for others by means of telephone and the global computer network"); In re Reed Elsevier Properties Inc., 482 F.3d 1376, 82 USPQ2d 1378 (Fed. Cir. 2007) (LAWYERS.COM generic for "providing an online interactive database featuring information exchange in the fields of law, legal news and legal services"); In re Oppedahl & Larson LLP, 373 F.3d 1171, 71 USPQ2d 1370 (Fed. Cir. 2004) (PATENTS.COM merely descriptive of computer software for managing a database of records and for tracking the status of the records by means of the Internet).

A TLD is a top level domain, i.e., a URL.

9.0 CRITERIA FOR DESCRIPTIVENESS

The TMEP sets forth the criteria for descriptiveness:

Third party registrations. No dictionary listing. First or only user. Combined terms. More than one meaning. Picture or illustration. Foreign equivalents. Acronyms. Intended users. Phonetic equivalent. Laudatory terms. Telephone numbers. Domain names.

For example, the TMEP considers the word "American."

If "AMERICA" or "AMERICAN" appears in a phrase or slogan, the examining attorney must evaluate the entire mark to determine whether it is merely descriptive as laudatory or even incapable. In re Boston Beer Co. L.P., 198 F.3d 1370, 53 USPQ2d 1056 (Fed. Cir. 1999) (THE BEST BEER IN AMERICA so highly laudatory and descriptive as applied to beer and ale that it is incapable of acquiring distinctiveness); In re Carvel Corp., 223 USPQ 65 (TTAB 1984) (AMERICA'S FRESHEST ICE CREAM held incapable for ice cream); In re Wileswood, Inc., 201 USPQ 400 (TTAB 1978) (AMERICA'S BEST POPCORN! and AMERICA'S FAVORITE POPCORN! merely descriptive of unpopped popcorn). Typically, these marks primarily extol the quality or popularity of the goods or services and secondarily denote geographic origin. TMEP 1209.03(n).

The TMEP elucidates other merely descriptive phrases:

"National," "International," "Global," "Worldwide."

Function or purpose - Source or provider of goods and services

Retail store or distributor services - Slogans

Repetition of descriptive or generic term - Punctuation

Examples: "Best Beer in America", "National Rent a Fence" "Screenwipe," "La Lingerie," "Tires Tires Tires," "Ceasar! Ceaser!," "888 Patents" (phone number), "Hotels.com."

This can all be summarized in the categorization matrix:

Inherently Distinctive		Non-inherently Distinctive	No Distinctiveness
No Secondary Meaning Required		Secondary Meaning Required	No TM Distinctiveness
Arbitrary & Fanciful	Suggestive	Descriptive, Geographic, Personal Name	Generic

In summary, choosing a trademark is an important part of marketing a product. A trademark is a guarantee to the public as to the source of the goods. However, a trademark cannot remove a word from the English language.

4 WHAT CAN'T BE A TRADEMARK 2 SCANDALOUS TRADEMARKS

A trademark protects the public by apprising a purchaser of the source of the goods, which is a good thing. However, other considerations come into play when someone tries to trademark bad words. How are first amendment rights involved? Does the Lanham Act trump the first amendment? Was something that was a common and accepted usage decades ago fall from grace as a result of changing public attitudes? How are public attitudes determined? That is, who is insulted? This talk will try to shed some light on this unusual aspect of trademarks.

1.0 THE LANHAM ACT

Trademark law is enshrined in the Lanham Act.

Trademarks can be many things, as long as the trademark is an indication of the source of the goods. These can by words, symbols, color, sound, or combinations.

What cannot be a trademarks is set forth in 15 U.S.C. § 1052:

(a) Consists of or comprises immoral, deceptive, or scandalous matter; or matter which may disparage or falsely suggest a connection with persons, living or dead, institutions, beliefs, or national symbols, or bring them into contempt, or disrepute; or a geographical indication which, when used on or in connection with wines or spirits, identifies a place other than the origin of the goods and is first used on or in connection with wines or spirits by the applicant on or after one year after the date on which the WTO Agreement (as defined in section 3501(9) of title 19) enters into force with respect to the United States.

(b) Consists of or comprises the flag or coat of arms or other insignia of the United States, or of any State or municipality, or of any foreign nation, or any simulation thereof.

(c) Consists of or comprises a name, portrait, or signature identifying a particular living individual except by his written consent, or the name, signature, or portrait of a deceased President of the United States during the life of his widow, if any, except by the written consent of the widow.

(d) Consists of or comprises a mark which so resembles a mark registered in the Patent and Trademark Office, or a mark or trade name previously used in the United States by another and not abandoned, as to be likely, when used on or in connection with the goods of the applicant, to cause confusion, or to cause mistake, or to deceive: Provided, That if the Director determines that confusion, mistake, or deception is not likely to result from the continued use by more than one person of the same or similar marks under conditions and limitations as to the mode or place of use of the marks or the goods on or in connection with which such marks are used, concurrent registrations may be issued to such persons when they have become entitled to use such marks as a result of their concurrent lawful use in commerce prior to . . .

2.0 IN RE FOX, 702 F.3d 633

This case pertains to chocolate lollipops molded into the shape of a rooster. It was an Appeal from PTAB to the CAFC for refusal of Examiner to register her mark as being immoral, deceptive or scandalous. In re Fox, 702 F.3d 633 (Fed. Cir. 2012), Judge Dyk.

From the decision:

> This court and its predecessor have long assumed that the prohibition "is not an attempt to legislate morality, but, rather, a judgment by the Congress that [scandalous] marks not occupy the time, services, and use of funds of the federal government." In re [635] Mavety Media Grp. Ltd., 33 F.3d 1367, 1374 (Fed.Cir.1994) (quotation marks omitted). Because a refusal to register a mark has no bearing on the applicant's ability to use the mark, we have held that § 1052(a) does not implicate the First Amendment rights of trademark applicants.

The court then went on to define the concept of "Scandalous":

> The USPTO must demonstrate that the mark is shocking to the sense of truth, decency, or propriety; disgraceful; offensive; disreputable; ... giving offense to the conscience or moral feelings; ... [or] calling out [for]

condemnation . . . More concisely, and especially usefully in the context of this case, the USPTO may prove scandalousness by establishing that a mark is "vulgar." . . . This demonstration must be made "in the context of contemporary attitudes," "in the context of the marketplace as applied to only the goods described in [the] application," and "from the standpoint of not necessarily a majority, but a substantial composite of the general public." (Citations omitted).

The appellants used Webster Dictionary definitions of "cock"="rooster" and "sucker"="lollipop."

The determination that a mark comprises scandalous matter is a conclusion of law based upon underlying factual inquiries ... Factual findings of the Board are reviewed for the presence of substantial evidence... while its ultimate conclusion as to registrability is reviewed de novo. ... The burden of proving that the proposed mark is unregistrable under 15 U.S.C. § 1052(a) rests on the PTO. Id.

Fox first argues that the Board lacked substantial evidence to support its finding that her mark has a vulgar meaning. Properly interpreted, Fox argues, the literal element of her mark means only "rooster lollipop." ... So too the association of COCK SUCKER with a poultry-themed product does not diminish the vulgar meaning — it merely establishes an additional, non-vulgar meaning and a double entendre. This is not a case in which the vulgar meaning of the mark's literal element is so obscure or so faintly evoked that a context that amplifies the non-vulgar meaning will efface the vulgar meaning altogether. Rather, the mark is precisely what Fox intended it to be: a double entendre, meaning both "rooster lollipop" and "one who performs fellatio."

The Examiner was affirmed. The mark was scandalous on its face.

3.0 BOSTON RED SOX v. SHERMAN, 88 U.S.P.Q. 2d 1581 (T.T.A.B. 2008)

vs.

The Applicant, Brad Sherman sought registration for clothing in Class 25. The goods he listed included "Clothing, namely, shirts, T-shirts, under shirts, night shirts, rugby shirts, polo shirts, cardigans, jerseys, uniforms, athletic uniforms, pants, trousers, slacks, jeans, denim jeans, overalls coveralls, jumpers,, jump suits, shorts, boxer shorts, tops, crop tops, tank tops, halter tops," etc. etc. etc. The ITU was for over 100 goods.

The Boston Red Sox didn't think it was funny and filed an opposition. The three grounds of the opposition were:

1) That the mark consists of immoral and scandalous matter.

2) That the mark disparages opposer and/or brings it into disrepute.

3) That the mark falsely suggests a connection with the opposer.

1) Immoral or scandalous matter: The Applicant admitted that SEX ROD is intended to possess a sexual connotation. The Random House dictionary demonstrated that the term "rod" has a vulgar meaning. The New Oxford American Dictionary characterizes "rod" as vulgar slang for penis. That is, the Red Sox argued that SEX ROD was matter that would be considered vulgar to a substantial composite of the public when used on T-shirts and other items of apparel, including, in particular, goods intended for children and infants. The Red Sox submitted dictionary evidence defining the word "rod" as "Slang...b. Vulgar, the penis." In response, Applicant argued that it was only "sexually suggestive" and described his mark as a parody of the RED SOX stylized mark. According to Applicant, the mark "represents the clever yet sophomoric sense of humor that prevails in venues in which apparel bearing the SEX ROD Stylized mark would likely be worn,

e.g., ballparks, sports bars, and university campuses."

2) Disparagement: Section 2(a): "matter which may disparage or falsely suggest a connection with persons, living or dead, institutions, beliefs, or national symbols, or bring them into contempt, or disrepute." To establish disparagement, Opposer was required to prove two elements: (1) that the communication would be understood as referring to the plaintiff, and (2) that the communication would be considered offensive or objectionable by a reasonable person of ordinary sensibilities. Finding that Applicant had copied the form, style, and structure of Red Sox's corporate symbol, and that Applicant's mark was so visually similar to the original. The TTAB found: "Applicant has copied the form, style and structure of the Club's corporate symbol." "Applicant admits that the design of his mark is intended to refer to Opposer and to evoke the Club."

3) Connection with the Red Sox: No likelihood of confusion or false suggestion of a connection with Red Sox since the disparaging nature of the term would undermine such findings. Also, for the same reasons there was no false suggestion of a connection.

The kicker was the number of goods listed by Sherman. The Opposer argued that Sherman's claimed bona fide intent at the time of filing was suspect "on its face" because Applicant was an individual with no relevant experience, training, or business connections of record, and hiss application covered a wide array of apparel. The Opposer argued that there was nothing in the record to indicate that Applicant had any capacity to conduct a genuine commercial enterprise involving the manufacture and distribution of clothing. The TTAB found that Opposer had satisfied its initial burden of showing the absence of any documentary evidence regarding Applicant's bona fide intention to use the mark given Applicant's failure to submit any evidence, documentary or otherwise, to support his claimed bona fide intent to use the mark when the application was filed.

Opposition sustained.

4.0 IN RE OLD GLORY CONDOM CORP, 26 USPQ2d 1216 (TTAB 1993)

Can an American Flag condom be trademarked? Yes. Holding not scandalous OLD GLORY CONDOM CORP and design comprising the representation of a condom decorated with stars and stripes in a manner to suggest the American flag.

5.0 RELIGIOUS SENSIBILITIES

Religious sensibilities are dealt with under scandalous bar. Some examples are: MADONNA for wine, MESSIAS for wine and brandy, BUDDHA BEACHWARE for apparel, SENUSSI for tobacco, and MOONIES for dolls that drop their pants. These marks were all analyzed not under the disparagement clause, but under the standard for scandalous marks.

In 2010, the TTAB, in a case involving the mark KHORAN for wine, explicitly addressed this situation and suggested that the disparaging bar was more appropriate for religious marks. In re Lebanese Arak Corp., 94 U.S.P.Q.2d (BNA) 1215, 1216 (T.T.A.B. 2010) (denying the mark because it would disparage a substantial composite of Muslims).

6.0 THE WASHINGTON REDSKINS

We can start with the original Redskins song (which has since been changed):

Hail to the Redskins!

Hail, victory!

Braves on the warpath!

Fight for Old D.C.!

Scalp 'em, swamp 'um—We will take 'um big score

Read 'um, Weep 'um,

Touchdown! -- We want heap more

Fight on, fight on, Till you have won

Sons of Wash-ing-ton. Rah!, Rah!, Rah!

Native American leaders challenged REDSKINS trademark in the USPTO in 1992 to cancel all six marks that contained the word "redskins."

The Evidence included dictionary definitions, reference works, reference sources or derogatory use of the word and the teams own use of the word.

The TTAB ruled in 145 page opinion canceling all of the trademarks. Harjo v. Pro Football, Inc. 50 U.S.P.Q.2d 1705 (T.T.A.B. 1999).

The team appealed to District Court for D.C. arguing laches, since the marks had been registered fro as long as 25 years. Court held for laches, also insufficient disparagement. But the previous decision found laches did not apply in matters of broad public policy. Harjo v. Pro Football, Inc., 565 f.3d 880(D.C. Cir. 2009).

Younger Native Americans brought suit in 2006, petitioning TTAB, arguing reaching majority overcame any criticism of delay.

TTAB of the United States Patent and Trademark Office (USPTO) voted to cancel the six trademarks held by the team in a two-to-one decision that held that the term "redskins" is disparaging to a "substantial composite of Native Americans," and this is demonstrated "by the near complete drop-off in usage of 'redskins' as a reference to Native Americans beginning in the 1960s. TTAB Proceeding 92046185, June 18, 2014.

Pictures from decision:

WASHINGTON

REDSKINS

The disparagement test had two prongs. The first prong was disparagement at the time of registration. The second prong was whether the term was disparaging.

Conclusions:

- Secondary meaning as football team did not overcome the core meaning of Native American.

- Disparagement was found of a "substantial composite" of Native Americans (based on submitted evidence).

- Drop off in usage of "redskins" to refer to Native Americans was noted starting from 1960s.

- Preponderance of evidence shows "redskins" to be disparaging.

- Laches does not apply to a disparagement claim where the disparagement pertains to a group of which the individual plaintiff or plaintiffs simply comprise one or more members.

The decision for cancellation was granted.

Please note that this goes on and on. Subsequent events include the Washington redskins filing appeal on August 14, 2014. E.D. Virginia upholds cancellation on July 8, 2015. Summ. J Granted. Pro Football, Inc. v. Blackhorse et al., Case No. 1:14-cv-01043-GBL-IDD. Oct. 20, 2015, Pro Football files appeal with Court of Appeal for the Fourth Circuit. No. 15-1874.

7.0 SLANTS

This case is closely related to the Redskins. This pertains to the disparagement of Asian Americans with the slant that the Applicant was Asian American.

THE SLANTS was Simon Tam's Asian-American musical group of that name. This is the specimen from TESS:

The appeal was from a decision not to grant the mark.

The Examiner found the mark disparaging to people of Asian descent under 15 U..S.C. § 1052(a) ("§ 2(a)"). The application was abandoned and a second application filed without Asian motifs. It was again found disparaging.

The disparagement analysis: "A disparaging mark 'dishonors by comparison with what is inferior, slights, deprecates, degrades, or affects or injures by unjust comparison.'" Cites to Redskins.

Two Part Test:

(1) what is the likely meaning of the matter in question, taking

into account not only dictionary definitions, but also the relationship of the matter to the other elements in the mark, the nature of the goods or services, and the manner in which the mark is used in the marketplace in connection with the goods or services; and

(2) if that meaning is found to refer to identifiable persons, institutions, beliefs or national symbols, whether that meaning may be disparaging to a substantial composite of the referenced group.

The first part is the likely meaning. The likely meaning of the matter in question.

Dictionary definitions used: "a disparaging term for a person of East Asian birth or ancestry," J.A. 219 (The American Heritage Dictionary of the English Language), and "[a] person with slanting eyes, spec. one of Oriental descent," J.A. 234–36(Oxford English Dictionary).

What must be found is whether the meaning may be disparaging to a substantial composite of the referenced group. The Japanese American Citizens League described the term "slant," when used to refer to people of Asian descent, as a "derogatory term."

A First Amendment right was claimed.

"With respect to appellant's First Amendment rights, it is clear that the PTO's refusal to register appellant's mark does not affect his right to use it. No conduct is proscribed, and no tangible form of expression is suppressed. Consequently, appellant's First Amendment rights would not be abridged by the refusal to register his mark."

There was no violation of the equal protection clause. Term used in a disparaging matter – not on account of race.

USPTO Aff'd. In re Tam, 108 U.S.P.Q.2d 1305 (T.T.A.B. Sept. 26, 2013). See also In re Tam, 785 F.3d 567 (Fed. Cir. 2015).

As of publication of this book, the latest chapter of the Slants saga was a hearing before the United States Supreme Court on

January 17, 2017. Almost every member of the court indicated that the law was hard to reconcile with the First Amendment. Malcolm L. Stewart, a deputy solicitor general, said the trademark law does not bar any speech, as the Slants remain free to continue to use their name. However, Justice Elena Kagan asserted that even government programs may not discriminate based on speakers' viewpoints. "The point is that I can say good things about something, but I can't say bad things about something," she said of the law. "And I would have thought that that was a fairly classic case of viewpoint discrimination."

Judge Kennedy was also favoring the Slants' position. "We have a culture in which we have T-shirts and logos and rock bands and so forth that are expressing a point of view," he said. "They are using the market to express views." See New York Times, January 18, 2017.

Compare this to HEEB. HEEB was OK for a magazine. On the other hand HEEB not OK for clothing. Appl. 78558043.

8.0 CONCLUSION

Dictionary definitions alone may be sufficient to establish that a proposed mark comprises scandalous matter, where multiple dictionaries, including at least one standard dictionary, all indicate that a word is vulgar, and the applicant's use of the word is limited to the vulgar meaning of the word. Boulevard Entm't, 334 F.3d at 1341, 67 USPQ2d at 1478 (holding 1-800-JACK-OFF FREE and JACK OFF scandalous, where all dictionary definitions of "jack-off" were considered vulgar); In re Manwin/RK Collateral Trust, 111 USPQ2d 1311, 1314 (T.T.A.B. 2014) (finding dictionary definitions alone sufficient to make prima facie showing that mark MOMSBANGTEENS comprises vulgar matte) .

The Two Bars:

1) Scandalous or Immoral: "shocking to the sense of propriety; offensive to the conscience or moral feeling; or calling out for condemnation." McGinly, 660 F.2d at 486, 211 USPQ2d at 673. – Tests against the perceptions of a substantial composite of the general public.

2) Disparaging: Tests the mark against the perceptions of the targeted group.

9.0 REFERENCES

Registering Offense: The Prohibition of Slurs as

Trademarks, Christine Haight Farley, Washington College of Law 2014, http://digitalcommons.wcl.american.edu/facsch_legsrp

Watch your mark – navigating the prohibitions on immoral, scandalous and disparaging trademarks, Perry J. Viscounty et al., World Trademark Review, December/January 2014, www.worldtrademarkreview.com

https://en.wikipedia.org/wiki/Washington_Redskins_trademark_dispute

Section 2: Getting a Trademark

5 TYPES OF APPLICATIONS

Trademark applications in the United States are filed in the United States Patent and Trademark Office (USPTO) located just outside Washington D.C. in Alexandria, Virginia. In 2015 there were a total of 2,074,702 total active certificates of registration and 503,889 applications filed. These applications are examined by 456 trademark examining attorneys in 1915, up from 378 in 2011.

Applying to register a trademark with the USPTO begins a legal process. Legal requirements and deadlines must be met and fees may be required throughout the process. There are 5 types of trademark applications, referenced by their basis in the Trademark Act: Section 1(a) Use; Section 1(b) Intent-to-Use; Section 44(d) Foreign application; Section 44(e) Foreign registration; and Section 66(a) Madrid Protocol..

Use In Commerce – Section 1(a)

The first type is based on use in commerce, which is outlined in the timeline below.

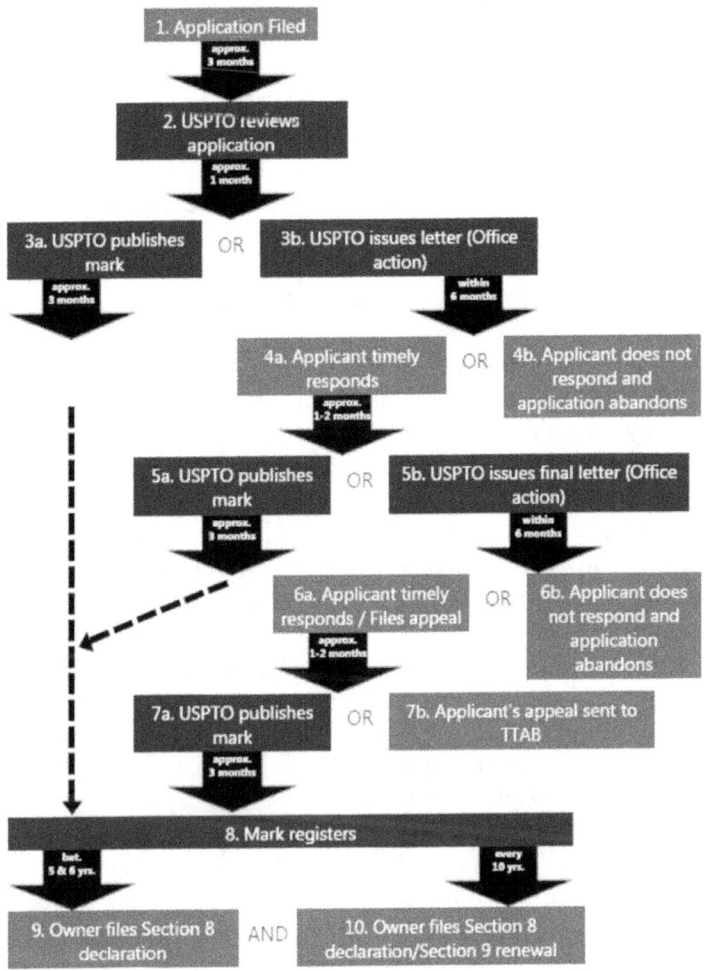

The steps in the process are as follows:

Step 1. Application filed: The filed application is assigned a serial number. This number should always be referenced when communicating with the USPTO.

Step 2. USPTO reviews application: If the minimum filing requirements are met, the application is assigned to an examining attorney. The examining attorney conducts a review of the application to determine whether federal law permits registration.

Step 3a. USPTO publishes mark: If no refusals or additional requirements are identified, the examining attorney approves the mark for publication in the Official Gazette (OG). The OG, a weekly online publication, gives notice to the public that the USPTO plans to issue a registration. Approximately 1 month after approval, the mark will publish in the OG for a 30-day opposition period. Any party who believes it would be harmed by the registration may file an objection (opposition) within that 30-day period with the Trademark Trial and Appeal Board.

Step 3b. USPTO issues letter (Office action): If refusals or requirements must still be satisfied, the examining attorney assigned to the application issues a letter (Office action) stating the refusals/requirements. The applicant must submit a response that addresses each refusal and requirement.

Step 4a. Applicant timely responds: In order to avoid abandonment of the application, the applicant must submit a timely response addressing each refusal and/or requirement stated in the Office action. The examining attorney will review the submitted response to determine if all refusals and/or requirements have been satisfied.

Step 4b. Applicant does not respond and application abandons: If the applicant does not respond within 6 months from the date the Office action was issued, the application is abandoned. The term "abandoned" means that the application process has ended and the trademark will not register.

Step 5a. USPTO publishes mark: If the applicant's response overcomes the refusals and/or satisfies all requirements, the examining attorney approves the mark for publication in the Official Gazette (OG). Approximately 1 month after approval, the mark will publish in the OG for a 30-day opposition period. Any party who believes it would be harmed by the registration may file an objection (opposition) within that 30-day period with the Trademark Trial and Appeal Board.

Step 5b. USPTO issues final letter (Office action): If the applicant's response fails to overcome the refusals and/or satisfy the outstanding requirements, the examining attorney will issue a "Final" refusal letter (Office action). The Office action makes "final" any remaining refusals or requirements. An applicant may respond to a final office action by a) overcoming the refusals and complying with the requirements or b) appealing to the Trademark

Trial and Appeal Board.

Step 6a. Applicant timely responds and/or files appeal: To avoid abandonment of the application, the applicant must submit a timely response addressing each refusal and/or requirement stated in the "Final" refusal letter (Office action). Alternatively, or in addition to the response, the applicant may also submit a Notice of Appeal to the Trademark Trial and Appeal Board (TTAB). The examining attorney will review the submitted response to determine if all refusals and/or requirements have been satisfied. If the applicant's response fails to overcome the refusals and/or satisfy the outstanding requirements, the application will be abandoned unless the applicant has filed a Notice of Appeal, in which case the application is forwarded to the TTAB.

Step 6b. Applicant does not respond and application abandons: If the applicant does not respond within 6 months from the date the Office action was issued and the applicant has not filed a Notice of Appeal to the Trademark Trial and Appeal Board, the application is abandoned.

Step 7a. USPTO publishes mark: If the applicant's response overcomes the refusals and/or satisfies all requirements of the "Final" refusal letter (Office action), the examining attorney approves the mark for publication in the Official Gazette (OG). The OG gives notice to public that USPTO plans to issue a registration. Approximately 1 month after approval, the mark will publish in the OG for a 30-day opposition period.

Step 8. Mark registers: If no opposition was filed, then the USPTO issues a registration. If an opposition was filed but it was unsuccessful, the registration issues when the Trademark Trial and Appeal Board dismisses the opposition.

Step 9. Registration owner files Section 8 declaration: Before the end of the 6-year period after the registration date, or within the six-month grace period after the expiration of the sixth year, the registration owner must file a Declaration of Use or Excusable Nonuse under Section 8. Failure to file this declaration will result in the cancellation of the registration.

Step 10. Registration owner files Section 8 declaration/Section 9 renewal: Within one year before the end of every 10-year period after the registration date, or within the six-month grace period thereafter, the registration owner must file a Combined Declaration of Use or Excusable Nonuse/Application for Renewal under Sections 8 & 9.

Intent To Use (ITU) – Section 1(b)

The timeline for an intent to use (ITU) application is set forth below.

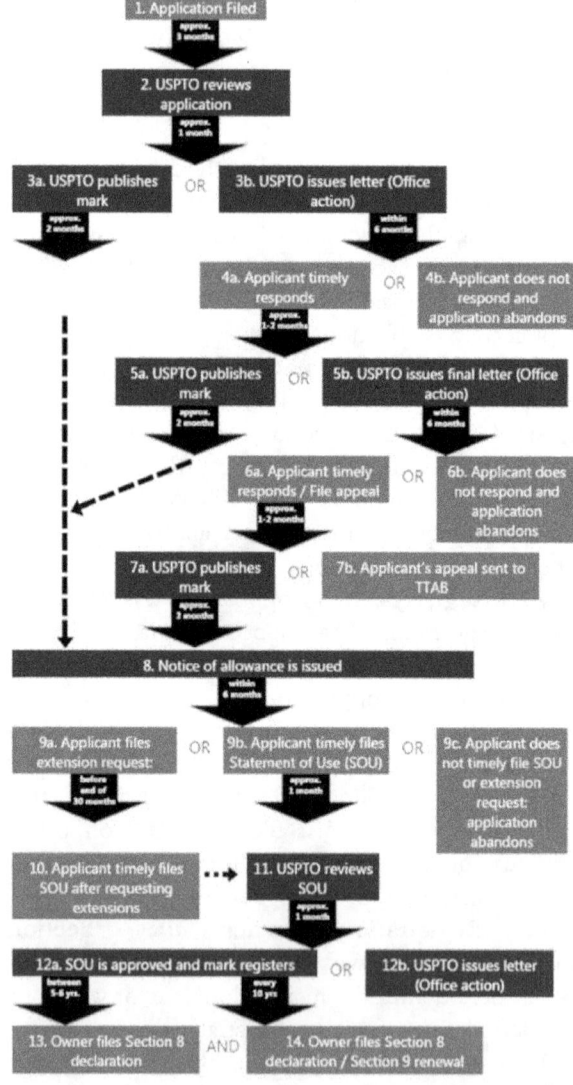

Step 1. Application filed: The filed application is assigned a serial number. This number should always be referenced when communicating with the USPTO. The applicant can check the status of any application throughout the entire process by entering the application serial number at http://tsdr.uspto.gov/ or by calling the trademark status line at 571-272-5400. Approximately 3 months go to step 1.

Step 2. USPTO reviews application: If the minimum filing requirements are met, the application is assigned to an examining attorney. The examining attorney conducts a review of the application to determine whether federal law permits registration. Filing fee(s) will not be refunded, even if the application is later refused registration on legal grounds. Approximately 1 month go to step 3a or step 3b.

Step 3a. USPTO publishes mark: If no refusals or additional requirements are identified, the examining attorney approves the mark for publication in the Official Gazette (OG). The OG, a weekly online publication, gives notice to the public that the USPTO plans to issue a registration. Approximately 1 month after approval, the mark will publish in the OG for a 30-day opposition period. Any party who believes it would be harmed by the registration may file an objection (opposition) within that 30-day period with the Trademark Trial and Appeal Board. No further action is taken until the opposition is resolved. Approximately 2 months go to step 8.

Step 3b. USPTO issues letter (Office action): If refusals or requirements must still be satisfied, the examining attorney assigned to the application issues a letter (Office action) stating the refusals/requirements. Within 6 months of the issuance date of the Office action, the applicant must submit a response that addresses each refusal and requirement. Within 6 months go to step 4a or step 4b.

Step 4a. Applicant timely responds: In order to avoid abandonment of the application, the applicant must submit a timely response addressing each refusal and/or requirement stated in the Office action. The examining attorney will review the submitted response to determine if all refusals and/or requirements have been satisfied. Approximately 1 to 2 months go to step 5a or step

5b.

Step 4b. Applicant does not respond and application abandons: If the applicant does not respond within 6 months from the date the Office action was issued, the application is abandoned. The term "abandoned" means that the application process has ended and the trademark will not register. Filing fees are NOT refunded when applications abandon. Abandoned applications are "dead," since they are no longer pending or under consideration for approval. To continue the application process, the applicant must file a petition to revive the application within 2 months of the abandonment date. If more than 2 months after the abandonment date, the petition will be denied as untimely and the applicant must file a new application with the appropriate fee(s).

Step 5a. USPTO publishes mark: If the applicant's response overcomes the refusals and/or satisfies all requirements, the examining attorney approves the mark for publication in the Official Gazette (OG). The OG, a weekly online publication, gives notice to the public that the USPTO plans to issue a registration. Approximately 1 month after approval, the mark will publish in the OG for a 30-day opposition period. Any party who believes it would be harmed by the registration may file an objection (opposition) within that 30-day period with the Trademark Trial and Appeal Board. No further action is taken until the opposition is resolved. Approximately 2 months go to step 8.

Step 5b. USPTO issues final letter (Office action): If the applicant's response fails to overcome the refusals and/or satisfy the outstanding requirements, the examining attorney will issue a "Final" refusal letter (Office action). The Office action makes "final" any remaining refusals or requirements. An applicant may respond to a final office action by a) overcoming the refusals and complying with the requirements or b) appealing to the Trademark Trial and Appeal Board. Within 6 months go to step 6a or step 6b.

Step 6a. Applicant timely responds and/or files appeal: To avoid abandonment of the application, the applicant must submit a timely response addressing each refusal and/or requirement stated in the "Final" refusal letter (Office action). Alternatively, or in addition to the response, the applicant may also submit a Notice of Appeal to the Trademark Trial and Appeal Board (TTAB). The examining attorney will review the submitted response to determine if all refusals and/or requirements have been satisfied. If the applicant\'s response fails to overcome the refusals and/or satisfy the outstanding requirements, the application will be abandoned unless the applicant has filed a Notice of Appeal, in which case the application is forwarded to the TTAB. The term "abandoned" means that the application process has ended and the trademark will not register. Filing fees are not refunded when applications abandon. Abandoned applications are "dead," since they are no longer pending or under consideration for approval. Approximately 1 o 2 months go to step 7a or step 7b.

Step 6b. Applicant does not respond and application abandons: If the applicant does not respond within 6 months from the date the Office action was issued and the applicant has not filed a Notice of Appeal to the Trademark Trial and Appeal Board, the application is abandoned. The term "abandoned" means that the application process has ended and the trademark will not register. Filing fees are not refunded when applications abandon. Abandoned applications are "dead," since they are no longer pending or under consideration for approval. To continue the application process, the applicant must file a petition to revive the application within 2 months of the abandonment date, with the appropriate fee. If more than 2 months after the abandonment date, the petition will be denied as untimely and the applicant must file a new application with the appropriate fee(s).

Step 7a. USPTO publishes mark: If the applicant's response overcomes the refusals and/or satisfies all requirements of the "Final" refusal letter (Office action), the examining attorney approves the mark for publication in the Official Gazette (OG). The OG, a weekly online publication, gives notice to the public that the USPTO plans to issue a registration. Approximately 1 month after approval, the mark will publish in the OG for a 30-day opposition period. Any party who believes it would be harmed by the registration may file an objection (opposition) within that 30-day period with the Trademark Trial and Appeal Board. No further action is taken until the opposition is resolved. Approximately 2 months go to step 8.

Step 7b. Applicant's appeal sent to TTAB: If the applicant's response does not overcome the refusals and/or satisfy all of the requirements and the applicant has filed a Notice of Appeal with the Trademark Trial and Appeal Board (TTAB), the appeal will be forwarded to the TTAB. Information about the TTAB can be found at www.uspto.gov.

Step 8. Notice of Allowance (NOA) is issued: A NOA is issued to the applicant within 2 months after the mark is published in the Official Gazette. The NOA is not a registration, but indicates that the mark will be allowed to register after an acceptable Statement of Use (SOU) is filed. The deadline for filing an SOU or request for extension of time (extension request) to file an SOU is calculated from the date the NOA issued. If the applicant does not file an SOU or extension request within 6 months of the date the NOA issued, the application will abandon. Within 6 months go to step 9a or step 9b or step 9c.

Step 9a. Applicant files extension request: If the applicant is not using the mark in commerce on all of the goods/services listed in the NOA, the applicant must file an extension request and the required fee(s) to avoid abandonment. Because extension requests are granted in 6 month increments, applicant must continue to file extension requests every 6 months. A total of 5 extension requests may be filed. The first extension request must be filed within 6 months of the issuance date of the NOA and subsequent requests before the expiration of a previously granted extension. Before the end of 30 months go to step 10.

Step 9b. Applicant timely files Statement of Use (SOU): If the applicant is using the mark in commerce on all of the goods/services listed in the NOA, the applicant must submit an SOU and the required fee(s) within 6 months from the date the NOA issued to avoid abandonment. Applicant cannot withdraw the SOU; however, the applicant may file one extension request with the SOU to provide more time to overcome deficiencies in the SOU. No further extension requests may be filed. Approximately 1 month go to step 11.

Step 9c. Applicant does not timely file SOU or extension request: application abandons: If the applicant does not file an SOU or extension request within 6 months from the date the Notice of Allowance issued, the application is abandoned (no longer pending/under consideration for approval). To continue the application process, the applicant must file a petition to revive the application within 2 months of the abandonment date.

Step 10. Applicant timely files SOU after requesting extensions: If the applicant is using the mark in commerce on all the goods/services listed in the NOA, the applicant must submit an SOU and the required fee(s) within 6 months from the previous extension to avoid abandonment. Applicant cannot withdraw the SOU; however, the applicant may file one extension request with the SOU to provide more time to overcome deficiencies in the SOU. No further extension requests may be filed. Go to step 11.

Step 11. USPTO reviews SOU: If the minimum filing requirements are met, the SOU is forwarded to the examining attorney. The examining attorney conducts a review of the SOU to determine whether federal law permits registration. The applicant cannot withdraw the SOU and the filing fee(s) will not be refunded, even if the application is later refused registration on legal grounds. Approximately 1 month go to step 12a or step 12b.

Step 12a. SOU is approved and mark registers: If no refusals or additional requirements are identified, the examining attorney approves the SOU. Within approximately 2 months after the SOU is approved, the USPTO issues a registration. To keep the registration "live," the registrant must file specific maintenance documents. Between 5 to 6 years go to step 13 and every 10 years go to step 14.

Step 12b. USPTO issues letter (Office action): If refusals or requirements must still be satisfied, the examining attorney assigned to the application issues a letter (Office action) stating the refusals/requirements. This is the same process that occurs prior to publication of the mark if the examining attorney determines that legal requirements must be met. The process and timeframes remain the same, except that if issues are ultimately resolved and the SOU is approved, the USPTO issues a registration within approximately 2 months. If all issues are not resolved, the application will abandon.

Step 13. Registration owner files Section 8 declaration: Before the end of the six-year period after the registration date, or within the six-month grace period after the expiration of the sixth year, the registration owner must file a Declaration of Use or Excusable Nonuse under Section 8. Failure to file this declaration will result in the cancellation of the registration.

Step 14. Registration owner files Section 8 declaration / Section 9 renewal: Within one year before the end of every 10-year period after the registration date, or within the six-month grace period thereafter, the registration owner must file a Combined Declaration of Use or Excusable Nonuse/Application for Renewal under Sections 8 and 9. Failure to make these required filings will result in cancellation and/or expiration of the registration.

Application Based On A Foreign Application – Section 44(d)

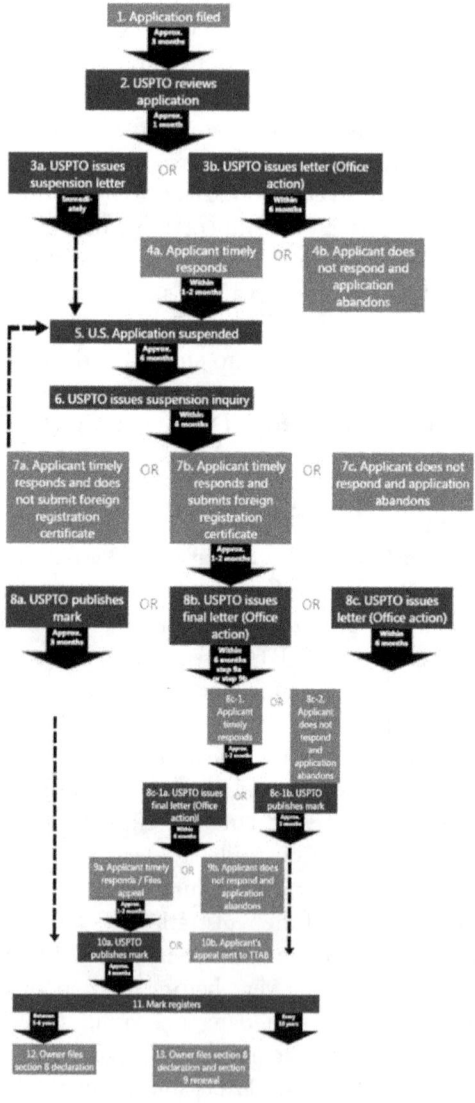

Step 1. Application filed: The applicant filed its U.S. application within 6 months of filing its foreign application in a country that is party to a treaty or agreement with the United States. The applicant's country of origin must also be a party to a treaty or agreement with the United States. However, the foreign application relied upon does not have to be from the applicant's country of origin. Section 44(d) alone does not provide a basis for publication or registration and the applicant must later provide a Section 1(b), Section 1(a), and/or Section 44(e) basis. Approximately 3 months go to step 2.

Step 2. USPTO reviews application: If the minimum filing requirements for the U.S. application are met, the application is assigned to an examining attorney to determine whether federal law permits registration. Filing fee(s) will not be refunded, even if the application is later refused registration on legal grounds. Approximately 1 month go to step 3a or step 3b.

Step 3a. USPTO issues suspension letter: If no refusals or requirements are identified, the examining attorney issues a letter suspending the action pending the submission of the foreign registration certificate and an English translation thereof. Go to step 5.

Step 3b. USPTO issues a letter (Office action): If the examining attorney identifies any refusals or requirements, the examining attorney issues a letter (Office action). Within 6 months of the issue date of the Office action, the applicant must submit a response that addresses each refusal and/or requirement. Within 6 months go to step 4a or step 4b.

Step 4a. Applicant timely responds: To avoid abandonment of the application, the applicant must submit a timely response addressing each refusal and/or requirement stated in the Office action. The examining attorney will review the submitted response and will issue a letter suspending the application pending submission of the foreign registration certificate and English translation thereof and continuing any refusals and/or requirements. No action by the applicant, other then periodic status checks every 3 – 4 four months of the U.S. application (see http://tsdr.uspto.gov), is required until the examining attorney issues a letter inquiring as to the status of the foreign application. Within 1 to 2 months go to step 5.

Step 4b. Applicant does not respond and application abandons: If the applicant does not respond within 6 months from the date the Office action issued, the application is abandoned. The term "abandoned" means that the application process has ended and the trademark will not register. Filing fees are not refunded when applications abandon. Abandoned applications are "dead," since they are no longer pending or under consideration for approval. To continue the application process, the applicant must file a petition to revive the application within 2 months of the abandonment date. If more than 2 months after the abandonment date, the petition will be denied as untimely and the applicant must file a new application with the appropriate fee(s).

Step 5. U.S. application suspended: No action by the applicant, other than periodic status checks every 3 – 4 months of the U.S. application (see http://tsdr.uspto.gov), is required. The application remains suspended until the examining attorney issues a letter inquiring as to the status of the foreign application. Approximately 6 months go to step 6.

Step 6. USPTO issues suspension inquiry: If the foreign registration certificate has not been submitted, the examining attorney will issue a letter inquiring as to the status of the foreign application. This cycle will continue every 6 months until the applicant submits its foreign registration certificate and English translation thereof. Within 6 months go to step 7a or step 7b or step 7c.

Step 7a. Applicant timely responds and does not submit foreign registration certificate: To avoid abandonment of the application, the applicant must submit a timely response indicating the status of the foreign application. If the foreign application is still pending, the examining attorney will issue a letter re-suspending the U.S. application. Go to step 5.

Step 7b. Applicant timely responds and submits foreign registration certificate: When the applicant has submitted its foreign registration certificate and English translation thereof, the U.S. application is removed from suspension and the examining attorney reviews the foreign registration to determine if the mark, owner, and goods/services agree with those in the U.S. application. Approximately 1 to 2 months go to step 8a or step 8b or step 8c.

Step 7c. Application does not respond and application abandons: If the applicant does not respond within 6 months from the date the Office action was issued, the application is abandoned. The term "abandoned" means that the application process has ended and the trademark will not register. Filing fees are not refunded when applications abandon. Abandoned applications are "dead," since they are no longer pending or under consideration for approval. To continue the application process, the applicant must file a petition to revive the application within 2 months of the abandonment date. If more than 2 months after the abandonment date, the petition will be denied as untimely and the applicant must file a new application with the appropriate fee(s).

Step 8a. USPTO publishes mark: The examining attorney approves the mark for publication in the Official Gazette (OG). The OG, a weekly online publication, gives notice to the public that the USPTO plans to issue a registration. Approximately 1 month after approval, the mark will publish in the OG for a 30-day opposition period, which may be extended upon request by a potential opposer. No further action is taken until the opposition period (including any extensions of time) has expired and any oppositions are resolved. Approximately 3 months go to step 11.

Step 8b. USPTO issues final letter (Office action): If the foreign registration certificate is acceptable but previously raised issues remain, the examining attorney will issue a "final" Office action to which the applicant must respond within 6 months, an applicant may respond to a final Office action by (a) overcoming the refusals and complying with the requirements, or (b) appealing to the Trademark Trial and Appeal Board. Within 6 months go to step 9a or step 9b.

Step 8c. USPTO issues letter (Office action): If the foreign registration is not acceptable, the examining attorney will issue a letter (Office action) to which the applicant must respond within 6 months. Within 6 months of the issue date of the Office action, the applicant must submit a response that addresses each refusal and/or requirement. Within 6 months go to step 8c-1 or step 8c-2.

Step 8c-1. Applicant timely responds: In order to avoid abandonment of the application, the applicant must submit a timely response addressing each refusal and/or requirement stated in the Office action. The examining attorney will review the submitted response to determine if all refusals and/or requirements have been satisfied. Approximately 1 to 2 months go to step 8c-1a or step 8c-1b.

Step 8c-2. Applicant does not respond and application abandons: If the applicant does not respond within 6 months from the date the Office action was issued, the application is abandoned. The term "abandoned" means that the application process has ended and trademark will not register. Filing fees are refunded when applications abandon. Abandoned "dead," since they no longer pending or under consideration for approval. To continue process, applicant must file a petition revive within 2 months of abandonment date. If more than after date, be denied as untimely new with appropriate fee(s).

Step 8c-1a. USPTO publishes mark: The examining attorney approves the mark for publication in the Official Gazette (OG). The OG, a weekly online publication, gives notice to the public that the USPTO plans to issue a registration. Approximately 1 month after approval, the mark will publish in the OG for a 30-day opposition period, which may be extended upon request by a potential opposer. No further action is taken until the opposition period (including any extensions of time) has expired and any oppositions are resolved. Within 6 months go to step 9a or step 9b.

Step 8c-1b. USPTO issues final letter (Office action): If the applicant's response fails to overcome the refusals and/or satisfy the outstanding requirements, the examining attorney will issue a "Final" refusal letter (Office action). The Office action makes "final" any remaining refusals or requirements. An applicant may respond to a final office action by a) overcoming the refusals and complying with the requirements or b) appealing to the Trademark Trial and Appeal Board. Approximately 3 months go to step 11.

Step 9a. Application timely responds / Files appeal: To avoid abandonment of the application, the applicant must submit a timely response addressing each refusal and/or requirement stated in the "final" Office action. Alternatively, or in addition to the response, the applicant may also submit a Notice of Appeal to the Trademark Trial and Appeal Board (TTAB). The examining attorney will review the submitted response to determine if all refusals and/or requirements have been satisfied. If the applicant's response fails to overcome the refusals and/or satisfy the outstanding requirements, the application will be abandoned unless the applicant has filed a Notice of Appeal, in which case the application is forwarded to the TTAB. The term "abandoned" means that the application process has ended and the trademark will not register. Filing fees are not refunded when applications abandon. Abandoned applications are "dead" since they are no longer pending or under consideration for approval. Approximately 1 to 2 months go to step 10a or step 10b.

Step 9b. Applicant does not respond and application abandons: If the applicant does not respond within 6 months from the date the Office action was issued, the application is abandoned. The term "abandoned" means that the application process has ended and the trademark will not register. Filing fees are not refunded when applications abandon. Abandoned applications are "dead," since they are no longer pending or under consideration for approval. To continue the application process, the applicant must file a petition to revive the application within 2 months of the abandonment date. If more than 2 months after the abandonment date, the petition will be denied as untimely and the applicant must file a new application with the appropriate fee(s).

Step 10a. USPTO publishes mark: If the applicant's response overcomes the refusals and/or satisfies all requirements, the examining attorney approves the mark for publication in the Official Gazette (OG). The OG, a weekly online publication, gives notice to the public that the USPTO plans to issue a registration. Approximately 1 month after approval, the mark will publish in the OG for a 30-day opposition period, which may be extended upon request by a potential opposer. No further action is taken until the opposition period (including any extensions of time) has expired and any oppositions are resolved. Approximately 3 months go to step 11.

Step 10b. Applicant's appeal sent to TTAB: If the applicant's response does not overcome the refusals and/or satisfy all of the requirements and the applicant has filed a Notice of Appeal with the Trademark Trial and Appeal Board (TTAB), the appeal will be forwarded to the TTAB. Information about the TTAB can be found at www.uspto.gov.

Step 11. Mark registers: Within approximately 3 months after the mark published in the Official Gazette (OG), if no opposition was filed, the USPTO issues a registration. If an opposition was filed but it was unsuccessful, the registration issues when the Trademark Trial and Appeal Board dismisses the opposition. After a registration issues, to keep the registration "alive," the registrant must file specific maintenance documents. Between 5 to 6 years go to step 12 or every 10 years go to step 13.

Step 12. Registration owner files section 8 declaration: Before the end of the 6-year period after the registration date, or within the 6-month grace period after the expiration of the sixth year, the registration owner must file a Declaration of Use or Excusable Nonuse under Section 8. Failure to file this declaration will result in the cancellation of the registration.

Step 13. Registration owner files section 8 declaration/section 9 renewal: Within 1 year before the end of every 10-year period after the registration date, or within the 6-months grace period thereafter, the registration owner must file a Combined Declaration.

Application Based on Foreign Registration – Section 44(e)

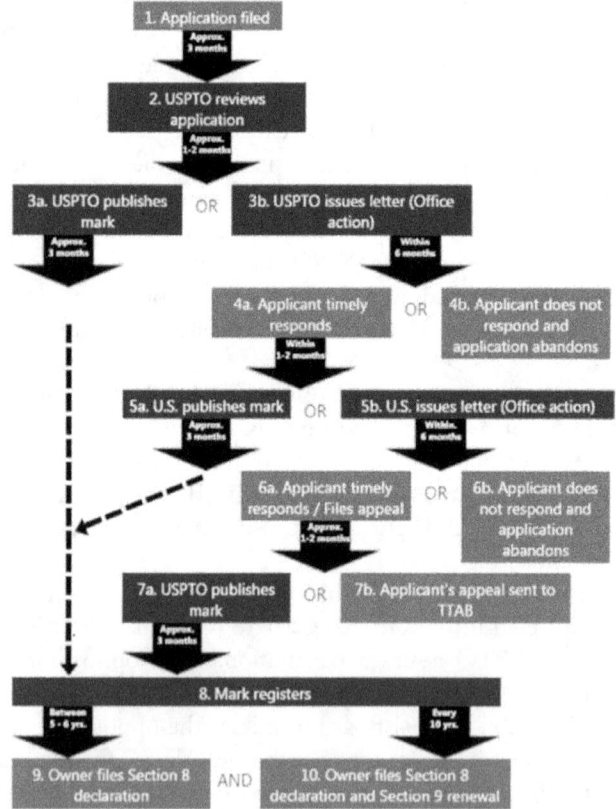

Step 1. Application filed: The applicant files its U.S. application and relies on ownership of a foreign registration. The foreign registration does not have to be submitted with the U.S. application, but when the foreign registration is submitted it should meet all of the following criteria: 1) issued by a country that is a party to a treaty or agreement with the United States; 2) from the applicant's country of origin; 3) owned by the applicant that filed the U.S. application; 4) the mark must be the same as the mark in the U.S. application; and 5) the goods/services must encompass the goods/services in the U.S. application. Approximately 3 months go to step 2.

Step 2. USPTO reviews application: If the minimum filing requirements for all applications are met, the application is assigned to an examining attorney who determines whether federal law permits registration. Filing fee(s) will not be refunded, even if the application is later refused registration on legal grounds. Approximately 1 to 2 months go to step 3a or step 3b.

Step 3a. USPTO publishes mark: If no refusals or additional requirements are identified and the foreign registration certificate and English translation thereof was included in the application, the examining attorney approves the mark for publication in the Official Gazette (OG). The OG, a weekly online publication, gives notice to the public that the USPTO plans to issue a registration. Approximately 1 month after approval, the mark will publish in the OG for a 30-day opposition period, which may be extended upon request by a potential opposer. No further action is taken until the opposition period (including any extensions of time) has expired and any oppositions are resolved. Approximately 3 months go to step 8.

Step 3b. USPTO issues letter (Office action): If refusals or requirements are identified the examining attorney issues a letter (Office action) requiring the applicant to address the issues. For example if the U.S. application does not meet the 44(e) requirements the applicant must either correct the deficiencies or provide another filing basis, such as Section 1a (use in commerce) or Section 1b (intent to use). Additionally, if the application fails to provide a foreign registration certificate, the examining attorney will require the application to submit a foreign registration certificate and English translation thereof. Applications are not suspended pending submission of a copy of the foreign registration certificate, unless the applicant establishes that it cannot obtain a copy of the foreign registration due to extraordinary circumstances (e.g., war or natural disaster). Within 6 months go to step 4a or step 4b.

Step 4a. Applicant timely responds: In order to avoid abandonment of the application, the applicant must submit a timely response addressing each refusal and/or requirement stated in the Office action. The examining attorney will review the submitted response to determine if all refusals and/or requirements have been satisfied. If an applicant fails to submit a copy of the foreign registration certificate in its response, the applicant has failed to respond to an outstanding requirement. Accordingly, the examining attorney will issue a "final" Office action. The Office action makes final any remaining refusals or requirements. An applicant may respond to a final office action by (a) overcoming the refusals and complying with the requirements, or (b) appealing to the Trademark Trial and Appeal Board. Within 1 to 2 months go to step 5a or step 5b.

Step 4b. Applicant does not respond and application abandons: If the applicant does not respond within 6 months from the date the Office Action was issued, the application is abandoned. The term "abandoned" means that the application process has ended and the trademark will not register. Filing fees are not refunded when applications abandon. Abandoned applications are "dead," since they are no longer pending or under consideration for approval. To continue the application process, the applicant must file a petition to revive the application within 2 months of the abandonment date. If more than 2 months after the abandonment date, the petition will be denied as untimely and the applicant must file a new application with the appropriate fee(s).

Step 5a. USPTO publishes mark: If the applicant's response overcomes the refusals and/or satisfies all requirements including the submission of the foreign registration certificate and English translation thereof, the examining attorney approves the mark for publication in the Official Gazette (OG). The OG, a weekly online publication, gives notice to the public that the USPTO plans to issue a registration. Approximately 1 month after approval, the mark will publish in the OG for a 30-day opposition period, which may be extended upon request by a potential opposer. No further action is taken until the opposition period (including any extensions of time) has expired and any oppositions are resolved. Approximately 3 months go to step 8.

Step 5b. USPTO issues final letter (Office action): If the applicant's response fails to overcome the refusals and/or satisfy the outstanding requirements, the examining attorney will issue a "Final" refusal letter (Office action). The Office action makes "final" any remaining refusals or requirements. An applicant may respond to a final office action by a) overcoming the refusals and complying with the requirements or b) appealing to the Trademark Trial and Appeal Board. Within 6 months go to step 6a or step 6b.

Step 6a. Applicant timely responds / Files appeal: To avoid abandonment of the application, the applicant must submit a timely response addressing each refusal and/or requirement stated in the "final" Office action. Alternatively, or in addition to the response, the applicant may also submit a Notice of Appeal to the Trademark Trial and Appeal Board (TTAB). The examining attorney will review the submitted response to determine if all refusals and/or requirements have been satisfied. If the applicant's response fails to overcome the refusals and/or satisfy the outstanding requirements, the application will be abandoned unless the applicant has filed a Notice of Appeal, in which case the application is forwarded to the TTAB. The term "abandoned" means that the application process has ended and the trademark will not register. Filing fees are not refunded when applications abandon. Abandoned applications are "dead," since they are no longer pending or under consideration for approval. Approximately 1 to 2 months go to step 7a or step 7b.

Step 6b. Applicant does not respond and application abandons: If the applicant does not respond within 6 months from the date the Office Action was issued, the application is abandoned. The term "abandoned" means that the application process has ended and the trademark will not register. Filing fees are not refunded when applications abandon. Abandoned applications are "dead," since they are no longer pending or under consideration for approval. To continue the application process, the applicant must file a petition to revive the application within 2 months of the abandonment date. If more than 2 months after the abandonment date, the petition will be denied as untimely and the applicant must file a new application with the appropriate fee(s).

Step 7a. USPTO publishes mark: Applicant has satisfied all the refusals and/or requirements. Accordingly, the examining attorney approves the mark for publication in the Official Gazette (OG). The OG, a weekly online publication, gives notice to the public that the USPTO plans to issue a registration. Approximately 1 month after approval, the mark will publish in the OG for a 30-day opposition period, which may be extended upon request by a potential opposer. No further action is taken until the opposition period (including any extensions of time) has expired and any oppositions are resolved. Approximately 3 months go to step 8.

Step 7b. Applicant's appeal sent to TTAB: If the applicant's response does not overcome the refusals and/or satisfy all of the requirements and the applicant has filed a Notice of appeal with the Trademark trial and Appeal Board (TTAB), the appeal will be forwarded to the TTAB. Information about the TTAB can be found at www.uspto.gov.

Step 8. Mark registers: Within approximately 3 months after the mark published in the Official Gazette (OG), if no opposition was filed, then the USPTO issues a registration. If an opposition was filed but it was unsuccessful, the registration issues when the Trademark Trial and Appeal Board (TTAB) dismisses the opposition. After a registration issues, to keep the registration "alive," the registrant must file specific maintenance documents. Between 5 to 6 years go to step 9 or every 10 years go to step 10.

Step 9. Owner Files Section 8 declaration: Before the end of the 6-year period after the registration date, or within the 6-month grace period after the expiration of the sixth year, the registration owner must file a Declaration of Use or Excusable Nonuse under Section 8. Failure to file this declaration will result in the cancellation of the registration.

Step 10. Owner files Section 8 declaration and Section 9 renewal: Within 1 year before the end of every 10-year period after the registration date, or within the 6-month grace period thereafter, the registration owner must file a Combined Declaration of Use or Excusable Nonuse/Application for Renewal under Sections 8 and 9. Failure to make these required filings will result in cancellation and/or expiration of the registration.

Application Based on the Madrid Protocol – Section 66(a)

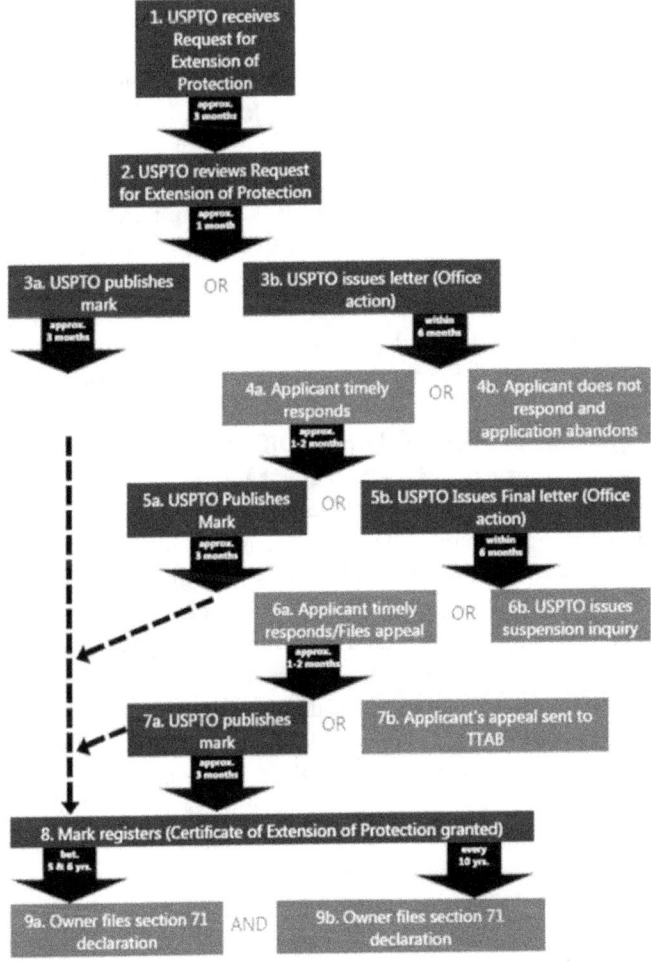

Step 1. USPTO receives Request for Extension of Protection: The World Intellectual Property Organization's International Bureau (IB) transmits the Request for Extension of Protection (REP) to the USPTO. The actual transmission to the USPTO could be weeks or months after the applicant's submission of the REP to its "Office of Origin." Applicants may not request protection directly, but must file such requests through a "home

country" intellectual property office.

Step 2. USPTO reviews Request for Extension of Protection: The Request for Extension of Protection is examined under the same standards as any other application for registration on the Principal Register. The USPTO examining attorney determines whether U.S. law permits registration. Filing fee(s) will not be refunded, even if the application is later refused registration on legal grounds.

Step 3a. USPTO publishes mark: If no refusals or additional requirements are identified, the USPTO examining attorney approves the mark for publication in the Official Gazette (OG). The OG, a weekly online publication, gives notice to the public that the USPTO plans to issue a registration. Approximately 1 month after approval, the mark will publish in the OG for a 30-day opposition period, which may be extended upon request by the potential opposer.

Step 3b. USPTO issues letter (Office action): If refusals and/or requirements exist, the USPTO examining attorney issues a letter (Office action, referred to by the International Bureau (IB) as a Provisional Refusal) explaining the refusals and/or requirements. This letter is sent to the IB, which forwards the action to the applicant. The refusal is either "total," meaning it applies to all goods/services/classes, or is "partial," meaning it applies to certain goods/services/classes. Within 6 months of the date the Office action was sent to the IB (USPTO mailing date), the applicant must submit a response to the USPTO that addresses each refusal and/or requirement in a "total" refusal. If the refusal is "partial," and the applicant does not respond within 6 months of the USPTO mailing date, the USPTO will abandon only those goods/services/classes refused and approve the mark for publication in the Official Gazette (OG).

Step 4a. Applicant timely responds: To avoid abandonment of the application, the applicant must submit a timely response addressing each refusal and/or requirement stated in the Office action. The examining attorney will review the submitted response to determine if all refusals and/or requirements have been satisfied. If the applicant's response fails to satisfy any of the refusals and/or requirements, the examining attorney will issue an Office action making any remaining refusals and/or requirements "final." An applicant may respond to a final Office action by (a) overcoming the refusals and complying with the requirements, or (b) appealing to the Trademark Trial and Appeal Board.

Step 4b. Applicant does not respond and application abandons: If the applicant does not respond within 6 months from the date the Office action was issued in a "total" refusal, the application is abandoned. If the refusal is "partial," and the applicant does not respond within 6 months of the USPTO mailing date, the USPTO will abandon only those goods/services/classes refused and approve the mark for publication in the Official Gazette (OG). See Step 5a USPTO publishes mark.

The term "abandoned" means that the application process has ended and the trademark will not register. Filing fees are not refunded when applications abandon. Abandoned applications are "dead," since they are no longer pending or under consideration for approval. To continue the application process, the applicant must file a petition to revive the application within 2 months of the abandonment date. Applications with partially abandoned goods/services/classes may petition to revive within 2 months of the date of the examiner's amendment abandoning/deleting those goods/services/classes. If more than 2 months after the abandonment date, the petition will be denied as untimely and the applicant must file a new application with the appropriate fee(s) or designate the United States for protection again in a "Subsequent Designation" of the International Registration of the mark.

Step 5a. USPTO publishes mark: If no refusals or additional requirements are identified, the USPTO examining attorney approves the mark for publication in the Official Gazette (OG). The OG, a weekly online publication, gives notice to the public that the USPTO plans to issue a registration. Approximately 1 month after approval, the mark will publish in the OG for a 30-day opposition period, which may be extended upon request by the potential opposer.

Step 5b. USPTO issues final letter (Office action): The examining attorney will issue a "final" Office action directly to the applicant or applicant's U.S. attorney. The Office action makes "final" any remaining refusals or requirements. The applicant may respond to a final Office action by (a) overcoming the refusals and complying with the requirements; (b) appealing to the Trademark Trial and Appeal Board; or (c) filing a petition to the Director in limited circumstances where review by the Director is allowed.

Step 6a. Applicant timely responds/Files appeal: To avoid abandonment of the application, the applicant must submit a timely response addressing each refusal and/or requirement stated in the "final" Office action. Alternatively, or in addition to the response, the applicant may also submit a Notice of Appeal to the Trademark Trial and Appeal Board (TTAB). The examining attorney will review the submitted response to determine if all refusals and/or requirements have been satisfied. If the applicant's response fails to overcome the refusals and/or satisfy the outstanding requirements, the application will be abandoned, either in "total" or in "part" if specified, unless the applicant has filed a Notice of Appeal, in which case the application is forwarded to the TTAB. The term "abandoned" means that the application process has ended and the trademark will not register. Filing fees are not refunded when applications abandon. Abandoned applications are "dead," since they are no longer pending or under consideration for approval. For goods/services/classes partially abandoned after "final" refusal, such goods/services/classes are no longer part of the application.

Step 6b. Applicant does not respond and application abandons: If the applicant does not respond within 6 months from the date the "final" Office action was issued, and the action does not specifically state that certain goods/services/classes will be "allowed" (or that certain goods/services/classes will be "deleted") if no reply is received, the entire application is abandoned. The term "abandoned" means that the application process has ended and the trademark will not register. Filing fees are not refunded when applications abandon. Abandoned applications are "dead," since they are no longer pending or under consideration for approval. To continue the application process, the applicant must file a petition to revive the application within 2 months of the abandonment date. If more than 2 months after the abandonment date, the petition will be denied as untimely and the applicant must file a new application with the appropriate fee(s) or designate the United States for protection again in a "Subsequent Designation" of the International Registration of the mark.

Step 7a. USPTO publishes mark: If no refusals or additional requirements are identified, the USPTO examining attorney approves the mark for publication in the Official Gazette (OG). The OG, a weekly online publication, gives notice to the public that the USPTO plans to issue a registration. Approximately 1 month after approval, the mark will publish in the OG for a 30-day opposition period, which may be extended upon request by the potential opposer.

Step 7b. Applicant's appeal sent to TTAB: If the applicant's response does not overcome the refusals and/or satisfy all of the requirements and the applicant has filed a Notice of appeal with the Trademark Trial and Appeal Board (TTAB), the appeal will be forwarded to the TTAB. Information about the TTAB can be found online at http://www.uspto.gov/trademarks/process/appeal/index.jsp.

Step 8. Mark registers (Certificate of Extension of Protection granted): Approximately 3 months after the mark is published in the Official Gazette (OG), if no opposition was filed, then the USPTO issues a certificate of registered extension of protection, referred to as a U.S. registration. If an opposition was filed but it was unsuccessful, the registration issues after the Trademark Trial and Appeal Board terminates the opposition.

Step 9a. Owner files Section 71 declaration: Between the 5th and 6th year after the date on which the USPTO issues the U.S. registration, or within the 6-month grace period with an additional fee, the holder of the international registration must file directly with the USPTO a Section 71 Affidavit of Use or Excusable Nonuse. Failure to file this declaration will result in the cancellation of the U.S. registration. The USPTO will then notify the International Bureau of the cancellation and invalidation of protection in the United States. The holder of the international registration may again designate the United States for protection in a "Subsequent Designation" of the international registration of the mark.

Step 9b. Owner files Section 71 declaration: Within 1 year preceding the end of every 10-year anniversary of the U.S. registration, or within the 6-month grace period with an additional fee, the holder of the international registration must file directly with the USPTO a Section 71 Declaration of Use or Excusable Nonuse. Failure to make these required filings will result in cancellation of the U.S. registration. The USPTO will then notify the International Bureau of the cancellation. In addition, to the USPTO maintenance requirements, the holder must also renew the international registration with the International Bureau every 10 years from the date of international registration (http://www.wipo.int/madrid/en/filing/renewal.html (link is external)). Failure to renew the international registration will result in cancellation by the International Bureau, which will notify all designated contracting parties that protection need no longer be afforded to the mark.

6 CLASSIFICATION AND SEARCH

A trademark informs the public of the source of goods and services. In order to obtain a trademark, the applicant must identify the goods and services to which the mark is to be associated. This is formalized in the Lanham Act in 15 U.S.C. § 1112, which sets forth the Classification of goods and services, and the registration in plurality of classes:

"The Director may establish a classification of goods and services, for convenience of Patent and Trademark Office administration, but not to limit or extend the applicant's or registrant's rights. The applicant may apply to register a mark for any or all of the goods or services on or in connection with which he or she is using or has a bona fide intention to use the mark in commerce: Provided, That if the Director by regulation permits the filing of an application for the registration of a mark for goods or services which fall within a plurality of classes, a fee equaling the sum of the fees for filing an application in each class shall be paid, and the Director may issue a single certificate of registration for such mark."

CLASSIFICATION

The classification is a number, and the number is based on the Nice (France) Agreement. The Nice Agreement groups products into 45 classes (classes 1-34 include goods and classes 35-45 embrace services), and allows users seeking to trademark a good or service to choose from these classes as appropriate. Since the system is recognized in numerous countries, this makes applying for trademarks internationally a more streamlined process. The classification system is specified by the World Intellectual Property Organization (WIPO).

The Nice Classifications are as follows:

GOODS

01: Chemicals used in industry, science and photography, as well as in agriculture, horticulture and forestry; unprocessed artificial resins, unprocessed plastics; manures; fire extinguishing compositions; tempering and soldering preparations; chemical substances for preserving foodstuffs; tanning substances; adhesives used in industry.

02: Paints, varnishes, lacquers; preservatives against rust and against deterioration of wood; colorants; mordants; raw natural resins; metals in foil and powder form for painters, decorators, printers and artists.

03: Bleaching preparations and other substances for laundry use; cleaning, polishing, scouring and abrasive preparations; soaps; perfumery, essential oils, cosmetics, hair lotions; dentifrices.

04: Industrial oils and greases; lubricants; dust absorbing, wetting and binding compositions; fuels (including motor spirit) and illuminants; candles and wicks for lighting.

05: Pharmaceutical and veterinary preparations; sanitary preparations for medical purposes; dietetic food and substances adapted for medical or veterinary use, food for babies; dietary supplements for humans and animals; plasters, materials for dressings; material for stopping teeth, dental wax; disinfectants; preparations for destroying vermin; fungicides, herbicides.

06: Common metals and their alloys; metal building materials; transportable buildings of metal; materials of metal for railway tracks; non-electric cables and wires of common metal; ironmongery, small items of metal hardware; pipes and tubes of metal; safes; goods of common metal not included in other classes; ores.

07: Machines and machine tools; motors and engines (except for land vehicles); machine coupling and transmission components (except for land vehicles); agricultural implements other than hand-operated; incubators for eggs; automatic vending machines.

08: Hand tools and implements (hand-operated); cutlery; side arms; razors.

09: Scientific, nautical, surveying, photographic, cinematographic, optical, weighing, measuring, signaling, checking (supervision), life-saving and teaching apparatus and instruments; apparatus and instruments for conducting, switching, transforming, accumulating, regulating or controlling electricity; apparatus for recording, transmission or reproduction of sound or images; magnetic data carriers, recording discs; compact discs, DVDs and other digital recording media; mechanisms for coin-operated apparatus; cash registers, calculating machines, data processing equipment, computers; computer software; fire-extinguishing apparatus.

10: Surgical, medical, dental and veterinary apparatus and instruments, artificial limbs, eyes and teeth; orthopaedic articles; suture materials.

11: Apparatus for lighting, heating, steam generating, cooking, refrigerating, drying, ventilating, water supply and sanitary purposes.

12: Vehicles; apparatus for locomotion by land, air or water.

13: Firearms; ammunition and projectiles; explosives; fireworks.

14: Precious metals and their alloys and goods in precious metals or coated therewith, not included in other classes; jewelry, precious stones; horological and chronometric instruments.

15: Musical instruments.

16: Paper, cardboard and goods made from these materials, not included in other classes; printed matter; bookbinding material; photographs; stationery; adhesives for stationery or household purposes; artists' materials; paint brushes; typewriters and office requisites (except furniture); instructional and teaching material (except apparatus); plastic materials for packaging (not included in other classes); printers' type; printing blocks.

17: Rubber, gutta-percha, gum, asbestos, mica and goods made from these materials and not included in other classes; plastics in extruded form for use in manufacture; packing, stopping and insulating materials; flexible pipes, not of metal.

18: Leather and imitations of leather, and goods made of these materials and not included in other classes; animal skins, hides;

trunks and travelling bags; umbrellas and parasols; walking sticks; whips, harness and saddlery.

19: Building materials (non-metallic); non-metallic rigid pipes for building; asphalt, pitch and bitumen; non-metallic transportable buildings; monuments, not of metal.

20: Furniture, mirrors, picture frames; goods (not included in other classes) of wood, cork, reed, cane, wicker, horn, bone, ivory, whalebone, shell, amber, mother-of-pearl, meerschaum and substitutes for all these materials, or of plastics.

21: Household or kitchen utensils and containers; combs and sponges; brushes (except paint brushes); brush-making materials; articles for cleaning purposes; steel wool; unworked or semi-worked glass (except glass used in building); glassware, porcelain and earthenware not included in other classes.

22: Ropes, string, nets, tents, awnings, tarpaulins, sails, sacks and bags (not included in other classes); padding and stuffing materials (except of rubber or plastics); raw fibrous textile materials.

23: Yarns and threads, for textile use.

24: Textiles and textile goods, not included in other classes; bed covers; table covers.

25: Clothing, footwear, headgear.

26: Lace and embroidery, ribbons and braid; buttons, hooks and eyes, pins and needles; artificial flowers.

27: Carpets, rugs, mats and matting, linoleum and other materials for covering existing floors; wall hangings (non-textile).

28: Games and playthings; gymnastic and sporting articles not included in other classes; decorations for Christmas trees.

29: Meat, fish, poultry and game; meat extracts; preserved, frozen, dried and cooked fruits and vegetables; jellies, jams, compotes; eggs; milk and milk products; edible oils and fats.

30: Coffee, tea, cocoa and artificial coffee; rice; tapioca and sago; flour and preparations made from cereals; bread, pastry and confectionery; ices; sugar, honey, treacle; yeast, baking-powder; salt; mustard; vinegar, sauces (condiments); spices; ice.

31: Grains and agricultural, horticultural and forestry products not included in other classes; live animals; fresh fruits and vegetables; seeds; natural plants and flowers; foodstuffs for animals; malt.

32: Beers; mineral and aerated waters and other non-alcoholic beverages; fruit beverages and fruit juices; syrups and other preparations for making beverages.

33: Alcoholic beverages (except beers).

34: Tobacco; smokers' articles; matches.

SERVICES

35: Advertising; business management; business administration; office functions.

36: Insurance; financial affairs; monetary affairs; real estate affairs.

37: Building construction; repair; installation services.

38: Telecommunications.

39: Transport; packaging and storage of goods; travel arrangement.

40: Treatment of materials.

41: Education; providing of training; entertainment; sporting and cultural activities.

42: Scientific and technological services and research and design relating thereto; industrial analysis and research services; design and development of computer hardware and software.

43: Services for providing food and drink; temporary accommodation.

44: Medical services; veterinary services; hygienic and beauty care for human beings or animals; agriculture, horticulture and forestry services.

45: Legal services; security services for the protection of property and individuals; personal and social services rendered by others to meet the needs of individuals.

This is not a complete list. A more detailed list is available from WIPO at http://www.wipo.int/classifications/nice/en/

SEARCH

A prerequisite for getting trademark is that someone else does not already own the mark. There is no requirement for search before filing for a mark, but is highly recommended that you do so. The USPTO's trademark database can be searched to see if any mark has already been registered or applied for that is similar to your mark and used on related products or for related services. If this search finds a mark that might conflict with your mark, then check the status to see if the application or registration is still "live," since any "dead" mark cannot be used to block a new application.

A complete search will uncover all similar marks, not just those that are identical. Searching for trademark availability is not the same as searching to register a domain name. A domain name search may focus on exact or "dead on" hits, with no consideration given to similar names or use with related products and services. Basically, a domain address is either available or it is not. The trademark process is more complex than the domain name process. As part of the overall examination process, the USPTO will search its database to determine whether to refuse registration because a similar mark is already registered for related products or services (i.e., even identical marks may co-exist if used on goods or services not considered to be related in any way). The USPTO is in no position to offer advisory opinions on the availability of a mark prior to filing of an actual application.

The trademark search engine of the USPTO is called TESS (Trademark Electronic Search System). TESS is free and open to all users with internet access. TESS provides access to text and images of registered marks, and marks in pending and abandoned applications. TESS can be found on the internet at: http://tmsearch.uspto.gov/bin/gate.exe?f=tess&state=4804:9jnug x.1.1. Logging on to TESS will present you with several search options:

Select A Search Option

▶ Basic Word Mark Search (New User)
This option cannot be used to search design marks.

▶ Word and/or Design Mark Search (Structured)
This option is used to search word and/or design marks. NOTE: You must first use the Design Search Code Manual to look up the relevant Design Codes.

▶ Word and/or Design Mark Search (Free Form)
This option allows you to construct word and/or design searches using Boolean logic and multiple search fields. NOTE: You must first use the Design Search Code Manual to look up the relevant Design Codes.

Additional Search Options

▶ Browse Dictionary (Browse Dictionary)
This option browses all fields in the database unless you limit to a particular field. Results are returned in a dictionary-style (alphabetic) format.

▶ Search OG Publication Date or Registration Date (Search OG)
This option searches the Official Gazette for marks published or registered on a particular date.

For example, putting the term "Coca Cola" into the basic word search will yield 187 live and dead marks, the first few of which are below.

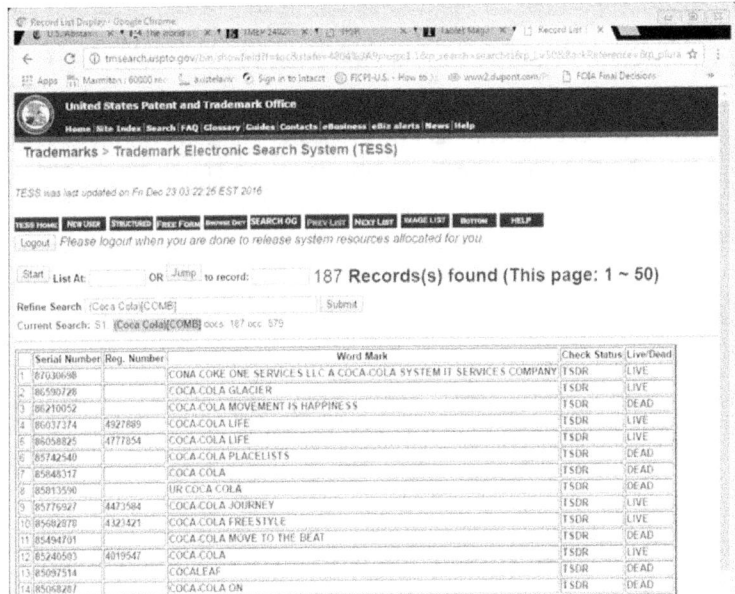

Clicking on the 12th hit for Coca Cola will yield the following:

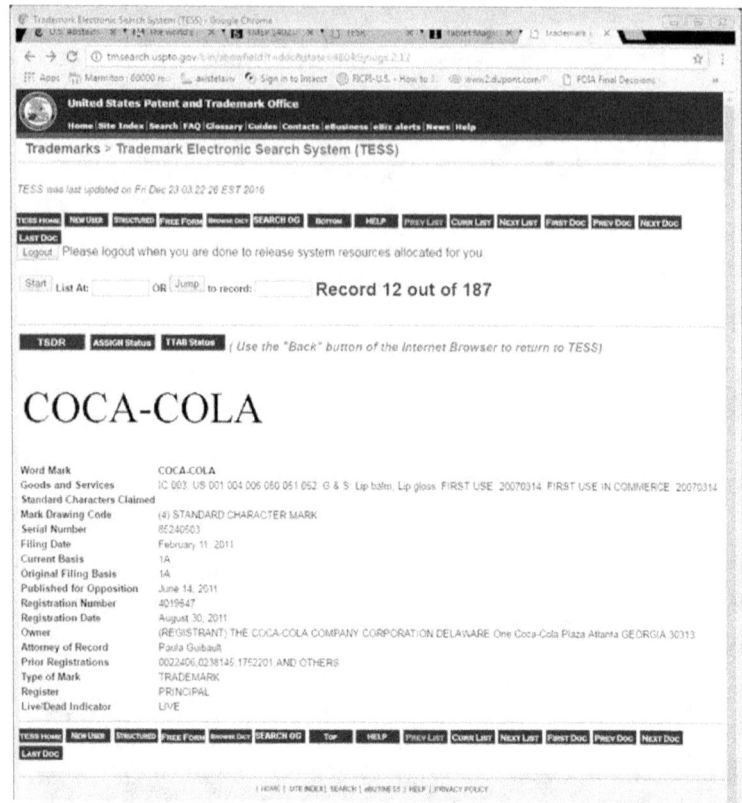

This gives the general data of the mark. Clicking on the TSDR button will take you to the entire prosecution history:

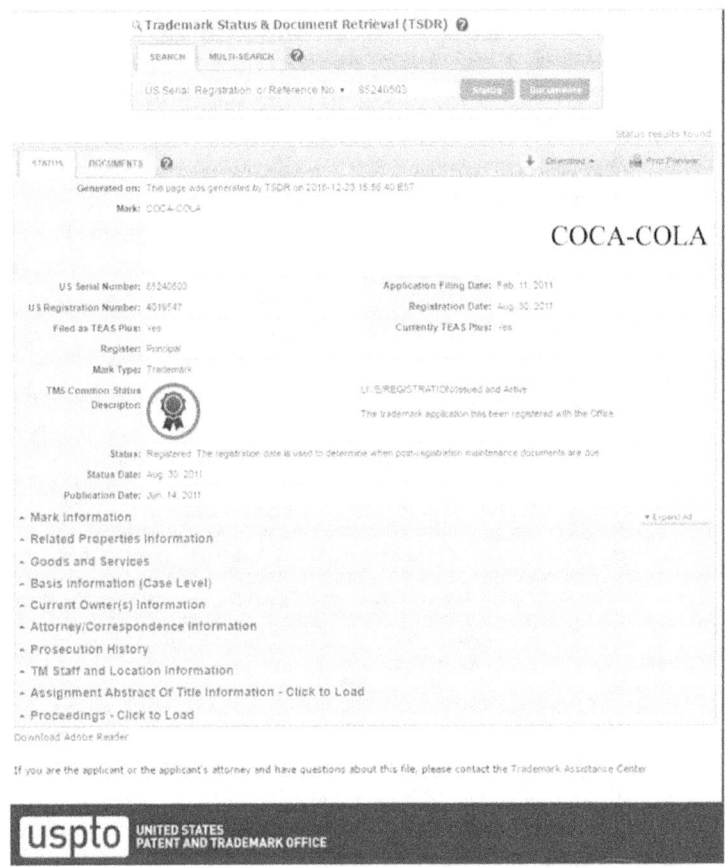

Another option is to search for designs in one of the advanced search options. TESS has a number code to categorize types of designs:

TABLE OF CATEGORIES

01   Celestial bodies, natural phenomena, geographical maps

This category includes objects that appear in the sky, including clouds, stars, moons, sun, planets and constellation. Additionally, designs associated with weather conditions such as rainbows, lightning, and snowflakes, maps of countries and continents.

02   Human beings

This category includes representations of men, women and children regardless of the activity they are engaged in or how they are dressed. Stylized humans, those in caricature form, stick figures and parts of the human body are also in this category.

03   Animals

This category includes most animals, except mythological animals. Animals found here include mammals, birds, kiwi, kiwi bird, fish, reptiles and insects. Prehistoric animals, stylized animals and animals with human attributes are also coded in category 03.

04   Supernatural beings, mythological or legendary beings, fantastical beings or unidentifiable beings

This category includes beings such as devils, angels, leprechauns, witches, and super heroes. Designs that are part human and part animal and mythological animals such as unicorns and Pegasus are in this category. Plants, objects or geometrical figures that represent humans or animals are also in category 04.

05   Plants

This category includes almost every type of plant such as flowers, trees, leaves, vegetables, and fruits. Also, decorations made from plants are in this category.

06   Scenery

This category includes mountains, lakes, waterfalls, beaches, forests and islands. Also, desert scenery and urban scenery such as skylines and street scenes fall within category 06.

07   Dwellings, buildings, monuments, stadiums, fountains, structural works and building materials

This category includes almost any structure that is built by man. All dwellings from igloos to skyscrapers are in 07. Interior and exterior portions of buildings along with building materials such as bricks, wood and cinderblocks are in this category.

08   Foodstuff

This category includes goods that are edible such as meat, dairy products, sandwiches, and baked goods. It does not include fruits and vegetables.

09   Textiles, clothing, headwear, footwear and sewing accessories

This category includes all types of clothing items and textile goods such as towels, curtains, sheets and carpeting. Also sewing products such as zippers, patterns, and sewing machines can be found in 09.

10   Tobacco, smokers' materials; fans; toilet articles; medical devices and apparatus including tablets, capsules or powders. This category includes most tobacco products and medical devices as well as products in tablet or capsule form. Grooming aids such as razors, toothbrushes, make up, non-motorized fans, canes and umbrellas in category 10.

11   Household utensils. This category includes most items that would be found in a household kitchen, including cutlery, cookware, beverage ware and electric or non-electric kitchen appliances. Other household utensils include irons, brooms and plungers.

12   Furniture and plumbing fixtures including all types of home and office furniture. Plumbing fixtures such as sinks, bathtubs and toilets are found in category 12.

13   Lighting, cooking, heating, cooling or refrigeration equipment, including lighting goods such as torches, candles, table lamps and flashbulbs. Stoves, refrigerators, toasters and air conditioners are also in category 13.

14   Hardware, tools and ladders; non-motorized agricultural implements; keys and locks, including all types of hardware, power tools and hand tools. Cables, wires, valves, hammers, locks, and non-motorized agricultural goods such as pitchforks, plows and rakes are in found here.

15   Machines and parts thereof, including industrial agricultural, home and office machines; electrical equipment, including all types of machines such as generators, conveyor belts, vacuum cleaners and vending machines. Office machinery such as computers, photocopiers, and cash registers can be found in category 15. Wheels and bearings are also in this category.

16   Telecommunications, sound recording or reproduction equipment; photography, cinematography and optics, including goods in the telecommunications and sound recording industries such as antennas, telephones, microphones, tape players, radios and televisions. Goods that are used for cinematography such as cameras and optical equipment, including eyeglasses and telescopes are in category 16.

17   Horological instruments and parts; jewelry; weights and measures, including all goods that measure time and all jewelry items. Additionally, scales such as the Scales of Justice are found here. Other measuring instruments such as rulers, thermometers

and Geiger counters are found in category 17.

18   Transport; equipment for animals; traffic signs, including all types of land, water and air vehicles, whether powered by animals, humans or motors. Equipment for animals such as saddles, leashes and horseshoes are found here. Traffic signs including stop signs, road signs and buoys are found in category 18.

19   Baggage, containers and bottles, including goods that are used to hold something such as luggage, barrels, bottles, boxes, coffins and baskets. Receptacles for laboratory use such as beakers and test tubes can be found in category 19.

20   Writing, drawing or painting materials, office materials, stationery and books, including most items found in a stationery store such as pencils, writing paper, labels and postage stamps. Books, magazines and newspapers are also found in category 20.

21   Games, toys and sporting articles, including all types of sporting equipment and toys such as dice, dolls, balls, toy hoops and swings. Merry-go-rounds and amusement park rides are also in category 21.

22   Musical instruments and their accessories; bells; sculptures, including any type of musical instrument such as guitars, bagpipes, whistles and tuning forks. Bells, including sleigh bells and the Liberty bell are found here. Any type of sculpture, whether of humans or animals can be found in category 22.

23   Arms, ammunition and armor, this category includes weapons, firearms, ammunition, and explosives such as fireworks and dynamite. Suits of armor are also found in category 23.

24   Heraldry, flags, crowns, crosses, arrows and symbols, including shields, crests and seals with or without words or figures. Coins, medals and prize ribbons can be found in category 24. Crowns, crosses and arrows have been classified here. Banners and flags, including any American flag, are included in this category. Lastly, symbols such as the dollar symbol, cent symbol, pound sterling symbol, yen symbol, euro symbol, percent symbol, punctuation marks and the universal prohibition symbol are in category 24.

25   Ornamental framework, surfaces or backgrounds with ornaments, including frames for pictures, ornamental borders and backgrounds such as checkerboards and wood graining. Designs consisting of repetitive figures, words and letters are found in category 25.

26 Geometric figures and solids, including includes geometric designs such as circles, triangles, rectangles, oblongs, polygons, ovals, diamonds, squares, quadrilaterals, lines, angles, chevrons, spheres, cubes, and prisms. It is the largest of all the categories.

27 Forms of writing, including designs that have letters, numbers, or punctuation symbols that are arranged in such a manner as to form a human, animal, plant or object. Conversely, if the design of a plant, human, geometric figure, or object is arranged to form a letter, number or punctuation symbol, they are found in category 27.

28 Inscriptions in various characters, including designs that have non-Latin characters. Inscriptions in Arabic, Chinese, Japanese, Hebrew and Greek are in this category.

29 Miscellaneous This category includes marks that consist solely of color. The codes for color marks are divided by the color, whether a single color or multiple colors are claimed, and whether the color is used over the entire object or only a portion of the object. Category 29 also includes inconspicuous design elements functioning as punctuation or parts of letters.

Each of these classifications has divisions. For example classification 27 for writing has sub-classifications such as 27.01 for letter or numerals forming figurative elements. 27.01.04   is for letters or numerals, including punctuation, forming representations of objects, parts of objects, or maps:

The Table of Categories can be found at http://tess2.uspto.gov/tmdb/dscm/index.htm.

An example of a word combined with a design category search would be to enter the code for American Indians (02.03.05) with the phrase "Land O Lakes" which would yield 42 records:

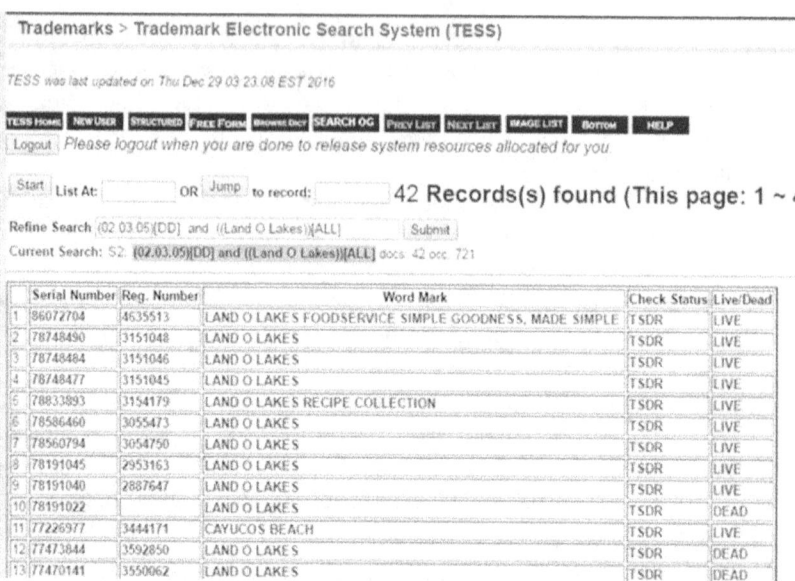

Trademarks > Trademark Electronic Search System (TESS)

TESS was last updated on Thu Dec 29 03:23:08 EST 2016

TESS HOME | NEW USER | STRUCTURED | FREE FORM | BROWSE DICT | SEARCH OG | PREV LIST | NEXT LIST | IMAGE LIST | BOTTOM | HELP

Logout Please logout when you are done to release system resources allocated for you.

Start List At: _____ OR Jump to record: _____ 42 Records(s) found (This page: 1 ~ 42

Refine Search (02 03 05)[DD] and ((Land O Lakes))[ALL]   Submit

Current Search: S2: (02.03.05)[DD] and ((Land O Lakes))[ALL] docs: 42 occ: 721

	Serial Number	Reg. Number	Word Mark	Check Status	Live/Dead
1	86072704	4635513	LAND O LAKES FOODSERVICE SIMPLE GOODNESS, MADE SIMPLE	TSDR	LIVE
2	78748490	3151048	LAND O LAKES	TSDR	LIVE
3	78748484	3151046	LAND O LAKES	TSDR	LIVE
4	78748477	3151045	LAND O LAKES	TSDR	LIVE
5	78833893	3154179	LAND O LAKES RECIPE COLLECTION	TSDR	LIVE
6	78586460	3055473	LAND O LAKES	TSDR	LIVE
7	78560794	3054750	LAND O LAKES	TSDR	LIVE
8	78191045	2953163	LAND O LAKES	TSDR	LIVE
9	78191040	2887647	LAND O LAKES	TSDR	LIVE
10	78191022		LAND O LAKES	TSDR	DEAD
11	77226977	3444171	CAYUCOS BEACH	TSDR	LIVE
12	77473844	3592850	LAND O LAKES	TSDR	DEAD
13	77470141	3550062	LAND O LAKES	TSDR	DEAD

A little exploring will yield the drawing:

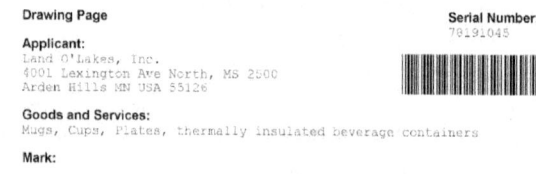

Drawing Page

Applicant:
Land O'Lakes, Inc.
4001 Lexington Ave North, MS 2500
Arden Hills MN USA 55126

Serial Number:
78191045

Goods and Services:
Mugs, Cups, Plates, thermally insulated beverage containers

Mark:

Going into great detail about the workings of TESS is beyond the scope of this book. However, it is advisable to learn how to use this database with proficiency.

7 FILING AND OFFICE ACTIONS

This chapter deals with the nuts and bolts of applying for and obtaining a trademark. Although not absolutely required, it is highly advisable to hire an attorney to who is familiar with trademark matters and the workings of the USPTO. Before ever filing a trademark application, a trademark attorney can conduct a more comprehensive search for potential problems with your use of a proposed mark than a layman will be able to conduct in TESS. The attorney then can counsel you regarding use of the mark, recommend whether to file a trademark application, and advise you on your likelihood of success in the registration process.

APPLYING ELECTRONICALLY

Trademark filings are accomplished electronically using the Trademark Electronic Application System (TEAS), which includes forms for the trademark application, maintenance and other trademark processes. The USPTO offers three versions of the electronic initial application form: TEAS Plus, TEAS Reduced Fee (TEAS RF), and TEAS Regular. TEAS Plus is the cheapest and most streamlined application. In exchange for completing all fields in the form marked with a red asterisk, selecting your listing of goods and services from the ID Manual, and agreeing to conduct correspondence electronically, you receive a heavily reduced filing fee. With TEAS RF, you do not have to file a complete initial application, but you must agree to conduct correspondence electronically. In exchange, you receive a moderately reduced filing fee. If you can't file a complete initial application and don't want to conduct correspondence electronically, you can file a TEAS Regular application, for the standard filing fee. This comparison chart will help you choose which initial application form is best.

Characteristics	TEAS Plus	TEAS Reduced Fee (TEAS RF)	TEAS Regular
Filing fee per class of goods/services	$225	$275	$325
E-mail address required for USPTO application-related correspondence	Yes	Yes	No
Additional submissions, like responses to Office actions, must be filed online	Yes	Yes	No
Goods/services listing must be selected from the USPTO Trademark Identification (ID) Manual	Yes	No	No
Full Filing fee paid upfront (per class for all classes listed on the application)	Yes	No	No
Certain statements regarding the mark be provided in the application as filed, if applicable (e.g. translation statement, claim of ownership color claim and description)	Yes - see TMEP §819.01	No	No
Additional processing fee if applicant does not satisfy the relevant filing option requirements	Yes - $50 per class of goods/services	Yes - $50 per class of goods/services	No

The electronic filing form in TEAS requires certain information, including the owner of the mark, the entity type, address of the owner, and contact information. The USPTO outlines the following steps:

STEP 1: If someone other than an attorney is filing the form, change the default setting for question #1 on the first page from Yes to No and click Continue.

STEP 2: Enter information in the appropriate fields in the form. You must enter information in all of the fields containing a red asterisk, as these fields are considered mandatory to receive an application filing date.

NOTE: To receive HELP at any point in the application process, simply click on any of the field names the appropriate HELP section will then be displayed at the bottom of your screen.

NOTE: If you did not enter information for a mandatory field, an "error" screen will pop up. For fields that are not considered mandatory, but for which an entry should be made, a "warning" screen will pop up. If necessary, you can by-pass a "warning" and move to the next section by clicking the "Continue" button.

STEP 3: If you are the proper signatory of the application, you will use the default "sign directly" option, wherein you will then sign the completed application by entering any combination of alpha/numeric characters that has been specifically adopted to serve the function of the signature, preceded and followed by a forward slash (/) symbol. Acceptable "direct' signatures could include, e.g., /john doe/ or /jd/. No "pre-approval" from the USPTO of the signature" is required, nor must the signature used even be consistent from one filing to the next.

If you are not signing directly, you must change the default setting to indicate either the "E-mail Text Form to second party for signature option" (the "e-signature approach) or the "Handwritten pen-and-ink signature option" (where you will mail/fax the application to the signatory for later upload of the signed declaration into the electronic form).

STEP 4: Upon completing the application, click on the "Validate Form" button at the end of the form. The validation function does not check the content of the entry for accuracy or completeness. The Pre-Examination section, and then later, the examining attorney, will determine the sufficiency and correctness of the entries.

STEP 5: Before submitting the application, double-check your work by clicking on the icons within the Validation Page (to view the application data in various formats):

Input: this presents the data in a simple "table" format (i.e., field name on the left, data on the right, with no "boilerplate" text).

Mark: the mark will appear in the middle of the page, either in the standard character format or as the JPEG image previously attached. You should determine that the entire mark is visible, in clear black-and-white (no gray tones), and not greater than 4x4 inches. (Because of different monitor settings, it is not always possible to determine this simply by viewing the image on-line.

Specimen: (only appears for a use-based application): the specimen image should be viewable.

XML File: this shows all of the data as associated with tagged data fields, which permits the USPTO to upload the information directly into our databases and avoid manual data entry errors.

Textform: this presents the application data in a narrative, paragraph-type format.

STEP 6: If any of the information being viewed is incorrect, you should close the page, to return to the main Validation Page. Then, click on the "Go Back to Modify" button at the bottom of the Validation Page, to return to the original application form. You can then correct any errors. Because a change has been made to the form, you must re-validate the application, again using the Validate Form button. At this point, you may resume the process at the Validation Page.

STEP 7: Enter the address(es) to which the USPTO should email the acknowledgment; e.g., a personal email address and/or a "docketing" email address specifically established to track application filings. The USPTO does not mail paper filing receipts for electronically submitted applications).

STEP 8: Re-enter the email address(es), to ensure delivery of the acknowledgment. (An inconsistent entry will result in a pop-up box asking for another entry of the address).

STEP 9: Read and check the box within the "Important Notice" section at the bottom of the Validation Page. This confirms an understanding that once an application is filed, we will not cancel the filing or refund the fee, unless the application fails to satisfy minimum filing requirements. The fee is a non-refundable processing fee.

STEP 10: To save the electronic file to a local drive, click on the "Download Portable Form" button at the bottom of the Validation Page.

STEP 11: Clicking on the PAY/SUBMIT button will bring up a

screen to enter the appropriate payment information. Shortly after successful transmission, a screen comes up that says "SUCCESS! We have received your application and assigned serial number _____." Again, within 24 hours, an email acknowledgment, containing both the assigned serial number and a complete summary of all data (but for any images), will also be sent to the email address provided at STEP 7. For your records, print out copies of the SUCCESS screen and the email acknowledgment.

STEP 12: If after successful filing an error is discovered, follow the steps outlined in the email acknowledgment for submission of a "Voluntary amendment."

TRACKING APPLICATION STATUS

The status of the prosecution of the application is tracked through the Trademark Status and Document Retrieval (TSDR) system at http://tsdr.uspto.gov. This is a simple form in which you can enter the serial number:

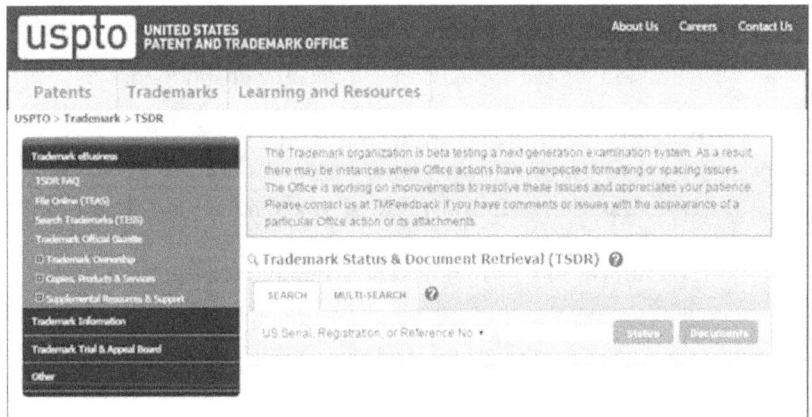

EXAMINATION AND OFFICE ACTIONS

USPTO Reviews Application

The USPTO first determines that the applicant has fulfilled the minimum filing requirements, an application serial number is assigned and the application is forwarded to an examining attorney. This may take months. The examining attorney reviews the application to determine whether it complies with all applicable rules and statutes, and includes all required fees. Filing fees will not be refunded. A complete review includes a search for conflicting marks and an examination the written application, the drawing, and any specimen.

USPTO Issues Letter (Office Action)

If the examining attorney decides that a mark is not registerable, he or she will issue a letter (Office action) explaining the substantive reasons for refusal, and any technical or procedural deficiencies in the application. If only minor corrections are required, the examining attorney may contact the applicant by telephone or email (if the applicant has authorized communication by email).

Applicant Timely Responds to Letter

After issuance of the Office action, the applicant must respond to the Office action within six (6) months of the mailing date of the Office action, or the application will become abandoned.

Possible Grounds for Refusal of a Mark

The common grounds for refusal of a mark are as follows:

Likelihood of Confusion: The Examiner conducts a search for conflicting marks. In evaluating an application, the Examiner searches USPTO records to determine whether there is a conflict between the mark in the application and a mark that is either registered or pending in the USPTO. The principal factors considered in reaching this decision are the similarity of the marks and the commercial relationship between the goods and services identified by the marks. To find a conflict, it is not required that the marks and the goods/services be exactly the same; instead, it is sufficient if the marks are similar and the goods and or services related such that consumers would mistakenly believe they come from the same source.

Similarity in sound, appearance, or meaning may be sufficient to support a finding of likelihood of confusion. The following are examples provided by the USPTO of marks that would be considered similar:

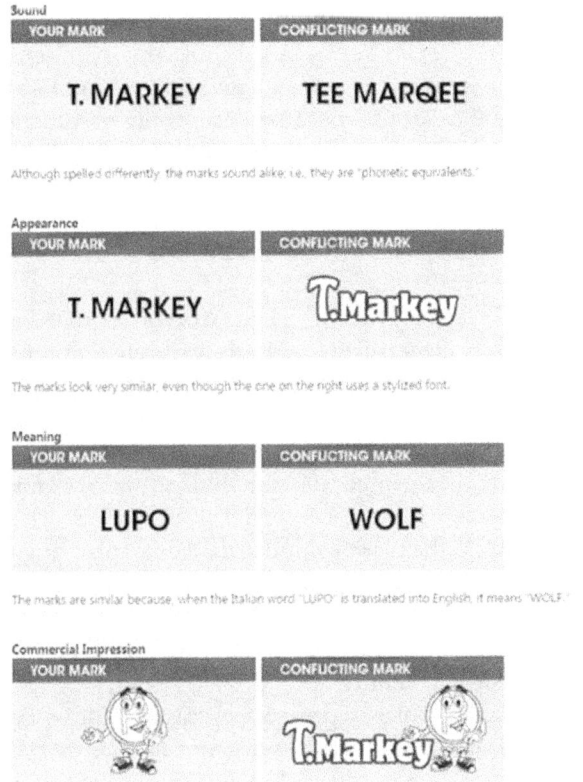

Many more examples can be found on the USPTO website at: https://www.uspto.gov/trademark/additional-guidance-and-resources/possible-grounds-refusal-mark.

Among the grounds for refusal of the mark include:

Merely Descriptive and Deceptively Misdescriptive: The mark is merely descriptive if it immediately describes an ingredient, quality, characteristic, function, feature, purpose or use of the specified goods or services. For example, the mark "CREAMY" would be merely descriptive for yogurt and the mark "WORLD'S

BEST BAGELS" would be merely descriptive for bagels.

A mark will be refused as deceptively misdescriptive if (1) the mark misdescribes an ingredient, quality, characteristic, function, feature, purpose or use of the specified goods or services; and (2) the misrepresentation conveyed by the mark is plausible. For example, the mark "THC Tea" would be deceptively misdescriptive of tea-based beverages not containing THC and the mark "SEPTEMBER 11, 2011" would be deceptively misdescriptive of history books and entertainment services not pertaining to the events of September 11, 2001.

For more information about merely descriptive and deceptively misdescriptive marks, see TMEP §§1209 et seq.

Primarily Geographically Descriptive and Primarily Geographically Deceptively Misdescriptive: A mark as primarily geographically descriptive if: (1) the primary significance of the mark is a generally known geographic location; (2) purchasers would be likely to think that the goods or services originate in the geographic place identified in the mark, i.e., purchasers would make a goods/place or services/place association; and (3) the mark identifies the geographic origin of the goods or services. For example, the mark "THE NASHVILLE NETWORK" would be primarily geographically descriptive of television program production and distribution services that originate in Nashville, Tennessee.

A mark is geographically deceptively misdescriptive if: (1) the primary significance of the mark is a generally known geographic location; (2) purchasers would be likely to think that the goods or services originate in the geographic place identified in the mark, i.e., purchasers would make a goods/place or services/place association; (3) the goods or services do not originate in the place identified in the mark; and (4) the misrepresentation would be a material factor in a significant portion of the relevant consumers' decision to buy the goods or use the services. For example, the mark "REAL RUSSIAN" would be primarily geographically deceptively misdescriptive for vodka that does not come from Russia.

For more information, see TMEP §§1210 et seq.

Primarily Merely a Surname: The mark has primary

significance to the public as a "surname", i.e., a family name or last name. For example, the mark "BINION'S" would be considered is primarily merely a surname. In addition, the mark "HAMILTON PHARMACEUTICALS" would be considered primarily merely a surname for pharmaceutical products. For more see TMEP §§1211 et seq.

Ornamentation: The mark is merely a decorative feature or part of the "dress" of the goods, i.e., merely ornamentation and does not serve the trademark function of identifying and distinguishing the applicant's goods from those of others.

With respect to clothing, consumers may recognize small designs or discrete wording as trademarks, rather than as merely ornamental features, when located, for example, on the pocket or breast area of a shirt. Consumers may not, however, perceive larger designs or slogans as trademarks when such matter is prominently displayed across the front of a t-shirt. For more information, see TMEP §§1202.03 et seq.

NOTE: For a complete list of the substantive grounds of refusal and a detailed explanation of each (including possible responses to a refusal), see Chapter 1200, Trademark Manual of Examining Procedure (TMEP).

APPEAL

If the applicant is not satisfied with the Examiner's rejection of the application, the application can be appealed. The Trademark Act gives applicants a right to appeal to the Board after a final action by an examining attorney. 15 U.S.C. §1070. Under 37 C.F.R. §2.141(a), a second refusal on the same grounds or a repeated requirement is considered a final action for purposes of appeal as long as all refusals or requirements are repeated in that action. Appeal from a first refusal or requirement, however, is premature.

The applicant must file the notice of appeal and appeal fee within six months of the date of issuance of the final refusal. 37 C.F.R. §2.142(a); TBMP §1202.02. For speediest consideration, file notices of appeal through the Electronic System for Trademark Trials and Appeals ("ESTTA") at http://estta.uspto.gov. Filing on paper slows down the process. If the applicant does not timely file a notice of appeal and appeal fee, the application is abandoned. 15

U.S.C. §1062(b). If the applicant's failure to file a proper notice of appeal was unintentional, the applicant may file a petition to revive

The applicant must file an appeal brief within 60 days of the date of the appeal, or the Board may dismiss the appeal.. The applicant's brief may not exceed twenty-five double-spaced pages in length, and should meet the requirements of 37 C.F.R. §2.126. 37 C.F.R. §2.142(b)(2); TBMP §1203.01. No evidence will be accepted after the filing of appeal. That is, the appeal is on the evidence on record.

After the applicant's brief has been filed, the Board will send a notice to the examining attorney. The examining attorney has sixty days from the date of the Board's notice to file a responsive brief with the Board and send a copy to the applicant. The TMEP contains a sample Examiner's appeal brief in Appendix A.

The applicant may file a brief in reply to the examining attorney's appeal brief. Reply briefs must be filed within twenty days of the date of issuance of the examining attorney's brief. 37 C.F.R. §2.142(b)(1). The examining attorney may not file a written response to the reply brief. However, in the oral argument (if the applicant requests an oral argument), the examining attorney should respond to any significant issues raised in the applicant's reply brief.

At the end of the appeal the Board may either affirm the examiner, reverse the Examiner or remand the application back to the Examiner for further prosecution in light of its decision.

OPPOSITION (TMEP 1503)

After examination of an application is completed and the examining attorney determines that the mark is entitled to registration on the Principal Register, the mark is published in the Official Gazette of the USPTO for opposition. A notice of opposition must be filed within thirty days after the date of publication, or within an extension of time granted by the Board for filing an opposition.

Any person who believes that he or she would be damaged by the registration of a mark on the Principal Register may file a notice of opposition with the Board, and paying the required fee, within thirty days after the date of publication, or within an extension period granted by the Board for filing an opposition. The notice of opposition must include a concise statement of the reasons for the opposer's belief that the opposer would be damaged by the registration of the opposed mark, and must state the grounds for opposition. Additional entities can join the opposition.

The Board has jurisdiction over the opposition. If the applicant files an amendment after a notice of opposition has been filed, the Board will act on it. After publication (and opposition) various types of amendment can be filed: restricting or deleting items in the existing identification, amendments to the classification of goods and services, amendments to marks, amendments to dates of use, amendments adding or deleting disclaimers, amendments to the basis, amendments to applicant's data.

REGISTRATION

At the successful conclusion of examiner, the trademark is registered, either as Principal Register registrations or Supplemental Register registrations. See TMEP §801.02(a) regarding the Principal Register, and TMEP §801.02(b) regarding the Supplemental Register.

In short, one of the requirements for a trademark registration is that the mark must be distinctive. Some trademarks are inherently distinctive, and these marks can be registered on the Principal Register as soon as a trademark application has worked through the application process. When a mark is placed on the Principal Register, the trademark owner is granted exclusive rights in the mark.

Marks which are capable of being protected but which are not inherently distinctive (principally descriptive marks) cannot be registered on the Principal Register until the trademark owner can show that the mark has acquired secondary meaning - that is, that the mark has acquired the requisite distinctiveness. Marks like this, that cannot be placed on the Principal Register because they are not inherently distinctive but which otherwise meet the qualifications for registration, can instead be placed on the Supplemental Register.

POST REGISTRATION

Once the trademark is registered, steps must be taken in order not to lose the mark. Required maintenance documents must be filed at regular intervals. Failure to file the required maintenance documents during the specified time periods will result in the cancellation of the U.S. trademark registration The factors include us and incontestability. ● Section71 declaration of use or excusable nonuse, filed between the 5th and 6th year after registration.

- Section 71 declaration of use or excusable nonuse.
- Section 7(d) request for new U.S. registration certificate.
- Voluntary surrender.
- Amendment and correction.
- Section 71 declaration of use or excusable nonuse: Between the 9th and 10th year after the registration date and every 10 years thereafter.
- Section 15 declaration of incontestability: A Section 15 declaration may be filed for a mark on the Principal Register that has been in continuous use in commerce for a period of 5 years after the date of the U.S. registration.

POST REGISTRATION TIMELINES

Post Registration Timelines

There are timelines for trademarks after registration. The timeline is the same for all marks except for those filed based on the Madrid Protocol.

The non-Madrid Protocol timeline:

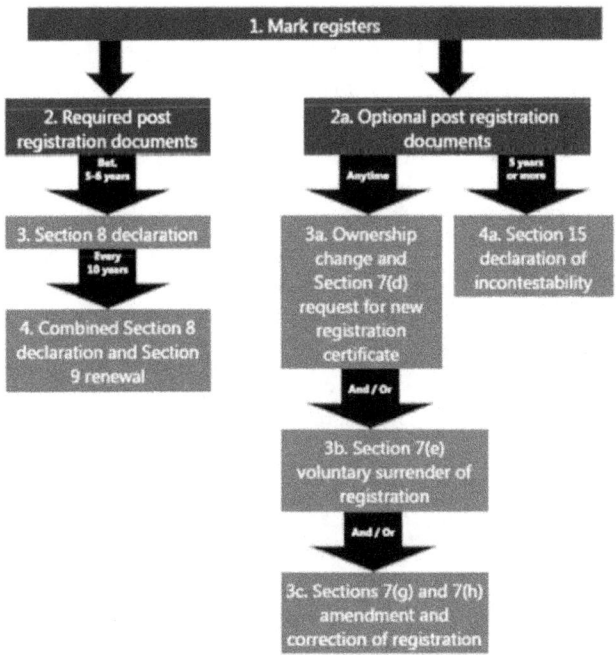

Step 1. Mark registers: After a registration issues, to keep the registration "alive" or valid, the registration owner must file specific documents and pay fees at regular intervals. The deadlines for filing these documents are calculated from the registration date shown on the registration certificate. Failure to file these documents will result in the cancellation and/or expiration of your registration. Go to step 2 for required post registration documents and go to step 2a for optional post registration documents.

Step 2. Required post registration documents: The following documents must be timely filed to maintain a registration. Go to step 3.

Step 2a. Optional post registration documents: The following documents are not mandatory to maintain a registration. For optional documents that may be filed anytime go to step 3a and for optional documents that may be filed every 5 years or more go to step 4a.

Step 3. Section 8 declaration: Between the 5th and 6th year after the registration date the owner must file a Declaration of Use or Excusable Nonuse under Section 8. This declaration requires a fee. The filing may also be made within a 6-month grace period after the expiration of the 6th year with the payment of an additional fee. Failure to file this declaration will result in the cancellation of the registration. The Section 8 declaration may be combined with an optional Section 15 declaration of incontestability. Go to step 4.

Step 3a. Ownership change and Section 7(d) request for new registration certificate: An owner may transfer or assign a registered mark to a new owner. The new owner is encouraged to record the assignment with the USPTO. If the owner would like a new registration certificate, the owner must submit a separate request showing that the assignment has been recorded with the USPTO. A fee is required. Go to Step 3b.

Step 3b. Section 7(e) voluntary surrender of registration: The owner of a registration may voluntarily surrender the registration, in its entirety or for a portion of the goods and/or services. No fee is required. Go to Step 3c.

Step 3c. Sections 7(g) and 7(h) amendment and correction of registration: A registration owner may file a Section 7 request to amend or correct the registration at any time. The amendment may not materially alter the mark or broaden the goods and/or services. A fee is required, except for corrections due to USPTO error.

Step 4. Combined Section 8 declaration and Section 9 renewal: Between the 9th and 10th year after the registration date and every 10 years thereafter, the owner must file a Combined Declaration of Use or Excusable Nonuse and Application for Renewal under Sections 8 and 9. This filing requires a fee. The filing may also be made within a 6-month grace period after the 10th year with the payment of an additional fee. Failure to file this declaration will result in the cancellation and/or expiration of the registration.

Step 4a. Section 15 declaration of incontestability: A Section 15 declaration may only be filed for a mark on the Principal Register that has been in continuous use in commerce for a period of 5 years after the date of the registration and there is no adverse decision(s) or pending proceeding(s) involving rights in the mark. "Incontestability" enhances the legal presumptions the registration receives. This declaration requires a fee.

The post-registration timeline for marks filed under the Madrid

Protocol is as follows:

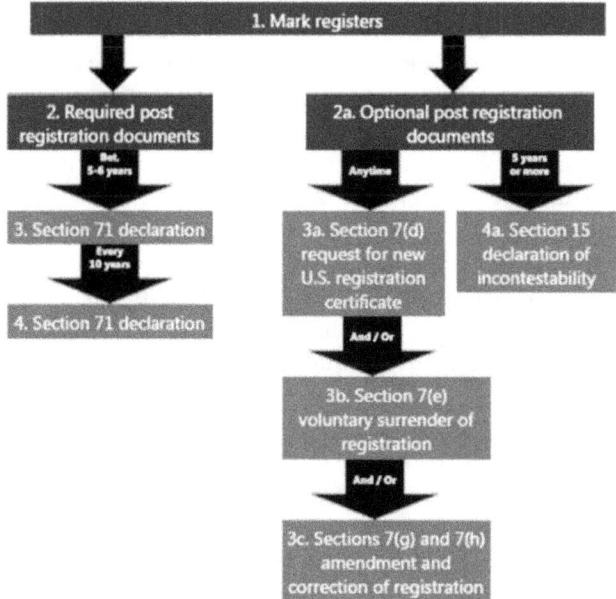

Step 1. Mark registers: After a U.S. registration issues, to keep the registration "alive" or valid, the U.S. registration owner must file specific documents and pay fees at regular intervals. The deadlines for filing Section 71 declarations of use and excusable nonuse are calculated from the registration date shown on the U.S. registration certificate. However, the deadlines for renewing the international registration with the International Bureau of the World Intellectual Property Organization are calculated from the international registration date. Failure to file both of these documents will result in the cancellation of your U.S. registration. Go to step 2 for required post registration documents and go to Step 2a for optional post registration documents.

Step 2. Required post registration documents: The following documents must be timely filed to maintain a registration. Go to Step 3.

Step 2a. Optional post registration documents: The following documents are not mandatory to maintain a registration. For optional documents that may be filed anytime go to Step 3a and for optional documents that may be filed every 5 years or more go to Step 4a.

Step 3. Owner files Section 71 declaration of use or excusable nonuse: Between the 5th and 6th year after the USPTO issues the U.S. registration, the U.S. registration owner must file directly with the USPTO a declaration of use or excusable nonuse. This declaration requires a fee and specimens of use. The filing may also be made within a 6-month grace period after the expiration of the 6th year with the payment of an additional fee. Failure to file this declaration will result in the cancellation of the U.S. registration and invalidation of the extension of protection of the international registration to the United States. Go to Step 4.

Step 3a. Section 7(d) request for new U.S. registration certificate: The owner of a registered extension of protection to the U.S. may only request a new U.S. registration certificate for the unexpired part of the registration period after filing the appropriate change request with the International Bureau of the World Intellectual Property Organization. Any change in ownership, such as by assignment, transfer, or change of name, must first be recorded at the International Bureau (IB). The IB will notify the USPTO of any changes of ownership that affect the extension of protection to the United States, including partial changes of ownership of less than all of the goods and/or services. The USPTO will update its electronic records to reflect the change. If the owner would like a new U.S. registration certificate, the owner must submit a separate request and pay the required fee. Go to Step 3b.

Step 3b. Section 7(e) voluntary surrender of U.S. registration: A U.S. registration owner may voluntarily surrender the U.S. registration, in its entirety or for a portion of the goods and/or services. No fee is required. Go to Step 3c.

Step 3c. Sections 7(g) and 7(h) amendment and correction of U.S. registration: A U.S. registration owner may file a request to amend or correct the U.S. registration at any time, but only in limited circumstances where the change will affect only the extension of protection to the United States. No amendments to the mark or to broaden the goods and/or services are allowed. A fee is required, except for corrections due to USPTO error.

Step 4. Owner files Section 71 declaration of use or excusable nonuse: Between the 9th and 10th year after the registration date and every 10 years thereafter, the U.S. registration owner must file directly with the USPTO a declaration of use or excusable nonuse. This declaration requires a fee and specimens of use. The filing may also be made within a 6-month grace period after the 10th year with the payment of an additional fee. Failure to file this declaration will result in the cancellation of the U.S. registration and invalidation of the extension of protection of the international registration to the United States. In addition, the international registration must be renewed with the International Bureau every 10 years from the date of international registration. Failure to file this renewal will result in the cancellation of the U.S. registration.

Step 4a. Section 15 declaration of incontestability: A Section 15 declaration may be filed for a mark on the Principal Register that has been in continuous use in commerce for a period of 5 years after the date of the U.S. registration and there is no adverse decision(s) or pending proceeding(s) involving rights in the mark. "Incontestability" enhances the legal presumptions the U.S. registration receives. This declaration requires a fee.

The required forms for trademark registration can be found online. Some examples are below:

Declaration of Use and/or Excusable Nonuse of a Mark under Section 8: https://teas.uspto.gov/postreg/sect08

Combined Declaration of Use of Mark in Commerce and Application for Renewal of Registration of a Mark under Section 8 & 9: https://teas.uspto.gov/postreg/s08n09

Declaration of Incontestability of a Mark under Section 15: https://teas.uspto.gov/postreg/sect15

Combined Declaration of Use and Incontestability Under Sections 8 and 15: https://teas.uspto.gov/postreg/s08n15

In conclusion, To keep a registration alive, the registration owner must file required maintenance documents at regular intervals. Failure to file the required maintenance documents during the specified time periods will result in the cancellation of the U.S. trademark registration or invalidation of the U.S. extension of protection.

SECTION 3 – DEFENDING YOUR TRADEMARK

8 INFRINGEMENT

Trademark infringement is the unauthorized use of a trademark or service mark on or in connection with goods and/or services in a manner that is likely to cause confusion, deception, or mistake about the source of the goods and/or services.

The basis for trademark infringement is found in §1114 of the Trademark Act 13 U.S.C. §114:

1) Any person who shall, without the consent of the registrant—

(a) use in commerce any reproduction, counterfeit, copy, or colorable imitation of a registered mark in connection with the sale, offering for sale, distribution, or advertising of any goods or services on or in connection with which such use is likely to cause confusion, or to cause mistake, or to deceive; or

(b) reproduce, counterfeit, copy, or colorably imitate a registered mark and apply such reproduction, counterfeit, copy, or colorable imitation to labels, signs, prints, packages, wrappers, receptacles or advertisements intended to be used in commerce upon or in connection with the sale, offering for sale, distribution, or advertising of goods or services on or in connection with which such use is likely to cause confusion, or to cause mistake, or to deceive,

shall be liable in a civil action by the registrant for the remedies hereinafter provided. Under subsection (b) hereof, the registrant shall not be entitled to recover profits or damages unless the acts have been committed with knowledge that such imitation is intended to be used to cause confusion, or to cause mistake, or to deceive.

A trademark owner who's mark is being infringed may file a civil action (i.e., lawsuit) in either state court or federal court for trademark infringement, depending on the circumstances. However, in most cases, trademark owners choose to sue for infringement in federal court. Even when a plaintiff chooses state court, it may be possible for the defendant to have the case "removed" to federal court.

If the trademark owner is able to prove infringement, available remedies may include the following:

▶ a court order (injunction) that the defendant stop using the accused mark;

▶ an order requiring the destruction or forfeiture of infringing articles;

▶ monetary relief, including defendant's profits, any damages sustained by the plaintiff, and the costs of the action; and

▶ an order that the defendant, in certain cases, pay the plaintiffs' attorneys' fees.

Conversely, a court may find instead that (1) you are not infringing the trademark, (2) a defense bars the plaintiff's claim(s), or (3) other reasons exist why the trademark owner is not entitled to prevail.

To support a trademark infringement claim in court, a plaintiff must prove that it owns a valid mark, that it has priority (its rights in the mark(s) are "senior" to the defendant's), and that the defendant's mark is likely to cause confusion in the minds of consumers about the source or sponsorship of the goods or services offered under the parties' marks. When a plaintiff owns a federal trademark registration on the Principal Register, there is a legal presumption of the validity and ownership of the mark as well as of the exclusive right to use the mark nationwide on or in connection with the goods or services listed in the registration. These presumptions may be rebutted in the court proceedings.

Generally, the court will consider evidence addressing a number of factors to determine whether there is a likelihood of confusion among consumers. The key factors considered in most cases are:

1. the degree of similarity between the marks at issue and whether the parties' goods and/or services are sufficiently related that consumers are likely to assume (mistakenly) that they come from a common source.

2. How and where the parties' goods or services are advertised, marketed, and sold;

3. The purchasing conditions.

4. the range of prospective purchasers of the goods or services.

5. Whether there is any evidence of actual confusion caused by the allegedly infringing mark.

6. the defendant's intent in adopting its mark; and the strength of the plaintiff's mark.

The particular factors considered in a likelihood-of-confusion determination, as well as the weighing of those factors, vary from case to case. And the amount and quality of the evidence involved has a significant impact on the outcome of an infringement lawsuit.

A trademark owner may also claim trademark "dilution," asserting that the owner owns a famous mark and the use of the defendant's mark diminishes the strength or value of the trademark owner's mark by "blurring" the mark's distinctiveness or "tarnishing" the mark's image by connecting it to something distasteful or objectionable-even if there is no likelihood of confusion.

GENERICIDE

When a trademark becomes generic and enters the English language, it is called genericide. This has happened to many trademarks: Escalator, Trampoline, Dry Ice, Linoleum, Nylon, Raison Bran, Yo Yo and Aspirin. Heroin was also once a trademark.

In the case deeming Aspirin generic in the United States, Judge Learned Hand set forth a standard for determining whether a mark has become generic:

"The single question, as I view it, in all these cases, is merely one of fact: What do the buyers understand by the word for whose use the parties are contending? If they understand by it only the kind of goods sold, them [sic], I take it, it makes no difference whatever what efforts the plaintiff has made to get them to understand more. He has failed, and he cannot say that, when the defendant uses the word, he is taking away customers who wanted to deal with him, however closely disguised he may be allowed to keep his identity." Bayer Co. v. United Drug Co., 272 F. 505, 509 (S.D.N.Y. 1921).

Trademark owners go to great lengths to protect their trademarks from going generic, for example Band-Aid, Scotch Tape or Xerox.

CYBERSQUATTING

The Anticybersquatting Consumer Protection Act ("ACPA") prohibits "cybersquatters" from registering internet domain names that are identical or confusingly similar to registered service marks and trademarks. See 15 U.S.C. § 1125(d)(1). The prohibition contained in § 1125(d)(1) applies when a domain name is identical or confusingly similar to a mark that is distinctive "at the time of registration of the domain name." This prevents people from registering a domain name that incorporates someone else's trademark and holding it for ransom.

However, there are free speech considerations. Consider People of Walmart at http://www.peopleofwalmart.com.

ACPA also permits in rem civil action to obtain forfeiture or cancellation of an infringing domain name.

EXCLUSIONS

The Lanham Act (15 U.S.C. §1125) sets forth the following exclusions:

"**Exclusions** The following shall not be actionable as dilution by blurring or dilution by tarnishment under this subsection:

(A) Any fair use, including a nominative or descriptive fair use, or facilitation of such fair use, of a famous mark by another person other than as a designation of source for the person's own goods or services, including use in connection with—

(i) advertising or promotion that permits consumers to compare goods or services; or

(ii) identifying and parodying, criticizing, or commenting upon the famous mark owner or the goods or services of the famous mark owner.

(B) All forms of news reporting and news commentary.

(C) Any noncommercial use of a mark."

The utilization of a trademark in comparative advertising is permissible. The Federal Trade Commission (FTC) policy sets forth: "Comparative advertising, when truthful and non-deceptive, is a source of important information to consumers and assists them in making rational purchase decisions. Comparative advertising encourages product improvement and innovation, and can lead to lower prices in the marketplace." However, disparaging advertising is not permitted. See FTC August 13, 1979 Statement of Policy Regarding Comparative Advertising, https://www.ftc.gov/public-statements/1979/08/statement-policy-regarding-comparative-advertising.

An example of disparagement was when a competitor altered the tractor maker John Deer's to show the deer running away. See Deere & Co. vs. MTD Products. 41 F.3d 39 (2nd Cir. 1994).

JOHN DEERE
Unaltered John Deere Logo.

Utilization of a trademark by a third party as a parody is also permissible. a parody must: (i) "convey two simultaneous—and contradictory—messages: that it is the original, but also that it is not the original and is instead a parody;" and (ii) "communicate some articulable element of satire, ridicule, joking, or amusement." See, e.g., People for the Ethical Treatment of Animals v.

Doughney, 263 F.3d 359, 366 (4th Cir. 2001). However, the parody must not create dilution, confusion, blurring, tarnishment or financial loss. See Patrick Emerson, "I'm Litigatin' It": Infringement, Dilution, and Parody Under the Lanham Act, 9 Nw. J. Tech. & Intell. Prop. 477, (2011). http://scholarlycommons.law.northwestern.edu/njtip/vol9/iss7/6.

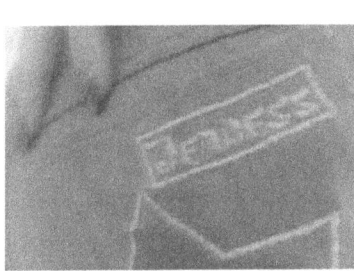

Gilda Radner's Jewess Jeans parodied Jordache Jeans in a SNL skit.

Starbucks hit back hard against "Dumb Starbucks." See Deborah J. Kemp, Lynn M. Forsythe & Ida M. Jones, Parody in Trademark Law: Dumb Starbucks Makes Trademark Law Look Dumb, 14 J. Marshall Rev. Intell. Prop. L. 143 (2015).

Use of a trademark in all forms of news reporting and news commentary is permissible. This is a first amendment right.

Noncommercial use of a trademark is also permissible.

Some examples of fair use include:

- use of a manufacturer's mark in the resale of goods, i.e., Ebay resales.

- artistic expression under the First Amendment in titles of artistic works such as movies and books.

- statements on repair shops such as "We repair BMW automobiles."

- cases for i-phones advertising "usable with i-phone 6."

COUNTERFEITING

15 U.S.C. §1127 (The Lanham Act) defines counterfeiting as: "A 'counterfeit' is a spurious mark which id identical with, or subsequently indistinguishable from, a registered mark."

One would think that counterfeiting is a straightforward topic. However, what about repair and rebuilding. At what point is a product repaired or rebuilt that it is no longer representative of the origin of the goods? One example is that a rebuilder of Rolex watches (with non-Rolex parts) resulted in a new product that was enjoined from bearing the Rolex trademark.

See Rolex Watch, U.S.A. v. Michel Co, 179 F.3d 704 (9th Cir. 1999).

9 REMEDIES

A trademark is representative of the owners reputation and goodwill. When a trademark is violated there is more involved than the costs of the goods or services provided by the violator of the trademarks. These damages can be difficult to quantify, and compensation with monetary damages often does not make the owner whole when the mark is infringed. There is therefore a wide range of remedies that should be considered when a trademark is being diluted, infringed or counterfeited.

The Lanham Act is the primary authority in trademark infringement cases. The Lanham Act gives the court power to grant injunctive relief (15 U.S.C. §1116(a) as well as permits plaintiffs to recover profits, damages and costs for violation of the Act's trademark provisions (15 U.S.C. §1117(a).

Injunctive Relief

An injunction limits or stops the use of an allegedly infringing mark. Frequently, the trademark violation is so egregious that damage is being cause to the mark holder before a decision at trial is reached. The trademark holder can therefore obtain a preliminary injunction.

A preliminary injunction is obtained early in a U.S. trademark infringement case. It limits or halts the use of an infringing mark prior to a final determination of the merits of the case. The grant of an injunction is an important form of relief and many times the primary remedy sought in a trademark infringement case.

Under the principles of equity, the party seeking a preliminary injunction must show that:

1. The plaintiff is likely to succeed on the merits of the case.

2. The plaintiff is likely to suffer irreparable harm in the absence of preliminary relief;

3. The balance of harms tips in the plaintiff's favor.

4. An injunction is in the public interest.

To establish irreparable harm, the moving party must demonstrate that other remedies, particularly monetary damages, are inadequate to compensate for the injury. In trademark infringement cases, U.S. courts traditionally have adopted a presumption of irreparable harm when a party demonstrates a likelihood of success on the merits of the case. Recent case law, however, has called into question the viability of this presumption of irreparable harm. This arose from and is a spillover from patent law, where non-practicing entities, i.e., patent trolls, sought injunctive relief. See eBay v. MercExchange, L.L.C., 547 U.S. 388 (2006).

Courts have found different types of evidence to be sufficient to demonstrate irreparable harm. Examples of evidence that may support irreparable injury include the following:

a) Evidence of a trademark owner's strong reputation and goodwill;

b) A particularly strong showing of likelihood of confusion;

c) Evidence of a threat to the trademark owner's reputation, potential business or goodwill;

d) Inability to control the nature and quality of the products sold or services offered by the infringer;

e) Evidence of actual confusion;

f) Evidence that the infringing mark is being used on an inferior product;

g) Evidence that the infringement impairs the trademark owner's ability to market its products or services;

h) Evidence that similar types of infringing conduct have led to significant confusion; and

i) Evidence of the non-moving party's inability to pay monetary damages.

Injunctive relief can also be sought following litigation. In this case, the main difference is that the plaintiff has succeeded on the merits of the case.

Monetary Damages

The Lanham Act permits recovery of damages, profits, costs and attorney's fees for trademark infringement. Standards for determining whether a plaintiff is entitled to a monetary award vary greatly between jurisdictions. Generally, plaintiffs are required to either demonstrate actual harm or present evidence of intentional, culpable or reckless conduct to be entitled to monetary relief.

Regarding damages, courts have recognized the liability doctrines of lost profits and unjust enrichment in order to make the plaintiff whole after a finding of trademark infringement.

The doctrine of lost profits permits the courts to determine the pecuniary cost to the plaintiff as a result of infringement. Recovery of actual damages normally requires plaintiff to demonstrate either actual consumer confusion as a result of the infringement, or that defendant's actions were intentionally deceptive. Actual injury may be proven by survey evidence, consumer data, market research, or evidence of diverted sales. Expert opinions by themselves are rarely convincing.

A defendant must disgorge all profits under the unjust enrichment theory, i.e., there must be zero gain. The award of profits does not depend on availability, or plaintiff's ability to prove, actual damages. In assessing profits the plaintiff shall be required to prove defendant's sales only. The defendant must prove all elements of cost or deduction claimed. Plaintiff is generally required to show willfulness of bad faith on the part of the defendant to recover defendant's profits.

That is, the plaintiff must be made whole. The courts have broad discretion to decrease or increase the reward.

The Lanham Act permits recovery of statutory damages for (a) use of counterfeit marks; and (b) cyberpiracy. Counterfeit marks carry a penalty of not less than $1.00 or more than $200.00 per counterfeit mark per type of goods or services sold, offered for sale or distributed. In the case of cyberpiracy, the plaintiff may elect, at any time before final judgment is rendered by the trial court, to recover, instead of actual damages and profits, an award of

Page 123

statutory damages in the amount of not less than $1,000 and not more than $100,000 per domain name.

In "exceptional cases" the Lanham Act permits attorney fees to the prevailing party. In this case, particularly egregious behavior must be demonstrated.

The Lanham Act does not permit punitive damages. However, there may be some remedy if the suit is under state law.

See Jura C. Zibas, Identifying new forms of "money" to satisfy monetary awards and strategies of defending against monetary relief and injunctions, AIPLA, Spring 2014 http://www.wilsonelser.com/writable/files/aipla_spring_2014_zib as.pdf.

Seizure of Goods

Section 1116 of the Lanham Act provides for the seizure of counterfeit goods. The court may, upon ex parte application, grant an order providing for the seizure of goods and counterfeit marks involved in a violation and the means of making such marks, and records documenting the manufacture, sale, or receipt of things involved in such violation. In this case a "counterfeit mark" means:

(i) a counterfeit of a mark that is registered on the principal register in the United States Patent and Trademark Office for such goods or services sold, offered for sale, or distributed and that is in use, whether or not the person against whom relief is sought knew such mark was so registered; or

(ii) a spurious designation that is identical with, or substantially indistinguishable from the mark.

The requirements for seizure include:

(A) the findings of fact and conclusions of law required for the order;

(B) a particular description of the matter to be seized, and a description of each place at which such matter is to be seized;

(C) the time period, which shall end not later than seven days after the date on which such order is issued, during which the seizure is to be made; and

(D) the amount of security bond required to be provided.

Any materials seized under the Act "shall be taken into the custody of the court," and the court must enter an appropriate protective order to cover any seized records.

Further details can be found in 15 U.S.C. §1116 (Section 34 of the Lanham Act).

Once the Ex Parte Seizure Order is issued by the court, the aggrieved party should identify the participants in the seizure and assemble a "team." Although the seizure itself is carried out by U.S. marshals or other law enforcement officers. The marshals cannot effectively execute the seizure without the assistance of others. The "team" usually includes trademark counsel. to provide direction to the seizure and address legal issues that are likely to arise during its course, such as the scope of the seizure.

Other potential participants in the seizure team include private investigators and/or photographers or videographers. Investigators can help the marshals or officers in identifying counterfeit goods or documents covered by the seizure order.

Seizure of goods can also be performed by the Federal Trade Commission (FTC) or by United States Customs under appropriate circumstances. For Example the U.S. Customs made 23,140 seizures in 2014. The breakdown is below:

FY 2014 Commodity	MSRP	Percent of Total*
Watches/Jewelry	$ 375,397,333	31%
Handbags/Wallets	$ 342,031,595	28%
Consumer Electronics/Parts	$ 162,209,441	13%
Wearing Apparel/Accessories	$ 113,686,295	9%
Pharmaceuticals/Personal Care	$ 72,939,399	6%
Footwear	$ 49,522,859	4%
Computers/Accessories	$ 26,652,422	2%
Optical Media	$ 18,780,989	2%
Labels/Tags	$ 17,675,452	1%
Toys	$ 8,178,351	Less than 1%
All Other Commodities	$ 39,273,404	3%
Total FY 2014 MSRP	$ 1,226,347,540	
Number of Seizures	23,140	

See https://www.cbp.gov/sites/default/files/documents/2014%20IPR%20Stats.pdf

ABOUT THE AUTHOR

Robert Goozner was born in New York City and grew up in Roosevelt New Jersey where he attended public school. He received a B.S. in Chemistry from the University of North Carolina, a Ph.D. in Chemistry from Temple University and a J.D. from George Mason University School of Law. He was a post-doctoral fellow at T.U. Clausthal and Uni Freiburg, both in Germany. His technical career included employment with Hoechst AG and Pall Corporation. Dr. Goozner won numerous Small Business Innovation Research (SBIR) grants in the fields of solar energy and waste disposal, and holds several patents in his own right. His subsequent career was spent practicing before the United States Patent and Trademark Office. Dr. Goozner has lectured extensively in the field of intellectual property. His is now a partner in the law firm of Young & Thompson in Alexandria, Virginia. The author also writes fiction in his spare time.

NOTES

NOTES